Praise for Simon Barnes's bestselling
How to be a bad birdwatcher

"A witty, perceptive book, thoughtful, instructive and full of simple wisdom." *Daily Mail*

"A delightful ode to the wild world outside the kitchen window... A book which fills you with that warm feeling that a shared love conquers all." *Daily Telegraph*

"*How to be a bad birdwatcher* is a work of pure enthusiasm for the cause of birds and us. Unstuffily, democratically, this book tries to help us derive good from things near at hand, everywhere, and it succeeds." *The Spectator*

"Ultimately, like all polemical texts, *How to be a bad birdwatcher* seeks to convert the reader to a cause. It does so with considerable success, and reveals that Barnes is neither a 'good' nor a 'bad' birdwatcher – simply a fulfilled and very lucky man." Stephen Moss, *Evening Standard*

"An amiable mix of memoir, the merits of binoculars, Charles Darwin, laughing gulls and how watching birds compares with his day job of watching England footballers." *The Observer*

A bad birdwatcher's
companion

A bad birdwatcher's companion

companion

...or a personal introduction to
Britain's 50 most obvious birds

SIMON BARNES

Illustrations by Peter Partington

✳ SHORT BOOKS

First published in 2005 by
Short Books
15 Highbury Terrace
London N5 1UP

10 9 8 7 6 5 4 3 2 1

A CIP catalogue record for this book
is available from the British Library.

Illustration copyright © Peter Partington

ISBN 1-904977-37-5

Printed in Great Britain by
William Clowes Ltd, Beccles, Suffolk

For WCB – with memories of coal tits,
Fullerborn's longclaw and Pearson's cisticola

Contents

Fresh water again

More Countryside

Pilgrimage birds

Foreword

A bad birdwatcher is me, a bad birdwatcher is you. A bad birdwatcher is anyone who looks at birds and feels a lift of the heart – but doesn't have to do anything about it. If you don't take accurate field notes; if you don't keep a bird diary; if you are a mite hazy on the differences between a first winter lesser black-backed gull and a second winter herring gull; if you don't know what a rachis is, still less a supercilium; if you don't own a telescope; and above all, if you don't keep lists, then you are a bad birdwatcher. That is to say, you are a bad birdwatcher if, despite not doing all these things, your heart still lifts at the sight of a good bird.

Many bad birdwatchers own a book about the

identification of birds, something called a field guide. Many don't. And many of those that do own one don't often open it. This is because a field guide, even the most generous and modest and straightforward, is a deeply intimidating object. It is too confusing. It contains too many birds. A bad birdwatcher simply doesn't know where to start.

Start here. Read this book, and be formally introduced to Britain's most obvious birds. And I hope, as you begin to know these 50 birds, that you will begin to understand them. Understand what they are doing out there and why: why there are so many different species, why some are bold and some are shy, why some are fierce and some are fearful, why some are bright and some are dull, why some are loud and some are quiet, why some are common and some are rare. I hope that, by reading this book, you will begin to understand the meaning of birds; and to realise that this is the most perfect and beautiful way towards the beginning of an understanding of the meaning of life.

And you can begin right now: by looking out of the window and seeing a bird. And feeling that lift of the heart.

Garden

1. Robin

But what does a red breast mean to a robin?

A red breast is not just the way a human can recognise a robin when it comes a-calling, or when it sits on a spade or a Christmas card. The red breast is not just a bit of chance colouration. No: the red breast is the core of the robin's being. The red breast is the love, the honour and the glory of a robin.

A robin is conspicuous because of its red breast. Have you noticed that a robin positively flaunts it? It is as if he is telling the world: "For God's sake, I'm a robin!"

It is quite clear, then, that the red breast doesn't just have a meaning for a birdwatchers. It also has a

Robin

Where to look: *gardens, spade handles, Christmas cards*
When to look: *all year*
What to look for: *red breast*
What to listen for: *thin, pretty song*

profound meaning for the bird. But he's not talking to birdwatchers. He's talking to robins.

And the red breast is how robins recognise each other: for love and for war. Both sexes have the red breast: both flaunt it. It can be a warning, it can be a come-on. Its meaning is both simple and complex, and at its heart is the statement: "I'm a robin! Deal with it!"

A robin stoked up to the eyeballs on the fevers of spring will react strongly to almost anything red. Robins have been observed attacking a bunch of red feathers. Chris Mead, a great ornithologist, noted robins displaying in response to his own spectacular red beard.

There is a 10 per cent chance that the robin who sits on your spade is a murderer. Perhaps even a far greater chance. Robins love to hold a territory, and they will defend it ferociously. Serious punch-ups involve pecking at eyes and legs. Robins can blind each other; and an estimated ten per cent of fights end up in death for one of the combatants.

That is not a reason to start calling robins vicious, or nasty. It is simply how robin society works. They operate by robin ethics, not human ethics. It is a tough world they live in, and only the best of them get to hold territory, breed, and produce young who will, in their turn, go on to breed. That, in brief, is the robin's goal in life; and, if you like, the goal of every other living thing on this planet.

Which is a pretty hefty conclusion to reach from the red breast of the robin redbreast – but it is inescapable. And the robin sings to further this ambition. A bird mostly sings to hold a territory, and most birds hold a territory only in spring when they breed; at other times of the year they adopt a different strategy. But the robin's game plan is to hold a territory throughout the year: a place where he, or she, can feed and stay safe, and survive throughout the hard weather.

And they announce their ownership in song. One of the joys of this, for us humans, is that it means they sing throughout the year. In the cold months, particularly at the end of the calendar year, one of the few birds you will hear singing is the robin: a sweet, thin, lisping song. Sentimentalists like to think that the song becomes more and more melancholy as the days grow darker.

This, quite apart from anything else, provides a perfect opportunity for a bad birdwatcher to learn a new bird song: almost everything you hear from late summer to Christmas will be a robin. Robins then make their seasonal irruption onto Christmas cards.

Why are robins so Christmassy? Because postmen – bringers of Christmas cards and presents – used to wear red jackets, and were called redbreasts. The uniform changes, but the bird still fulfils his symbolic Christmas role: flaunting that red breast against the snow, a gloriously encouraging sign of life in the most forbidding possible circumstances.

Young robins don't have red breasts, and so they are often overlooked – by birdwatchers, and by grown-up robins as well. That is a very smart move on the young robins' part. They don't try to hold a territory, they don't seek to challenge any grown-up, all they want is a quiet life until they are old enough, and brave enough, to want something different. And then the red breast will come.

A bird has its being in colour and sound, and this is one of the many reasons why humans relate so strongly to birds. Humans like robins for their brightness, their redness, their cheerfulness, for the wing-flicking, tail-twitching, chest-flaunting way they seem all to be such characters, for their confiding nature and the perky way they set about life. Robins actively seek humans out, when they are doing some robin-useful behaviour like digging. Oddly, outside Britain, robins are skulking and secretive birds, shy and seldom seen. Only in

Britain do they have this flamboyant trust in humans.

Robins are the birds that every one knows. But their lives are complex, passionate, violent, spectacular – at times desperate and sometimes glorious. When you see a robin, you see a red breast. But you see also the leading character in a strange and passionate drama.

Blackbird

Where to look: *lawns, gateposts*
When to look: *all year*
What to look for: *black and more
black, yellow beak*
What to listen for: *laid-back fluting,
mid to late spring*

2. Blackbird

A lawn isn't a lawn without a blackbird. It is one of the great sights of the suburban spring: the grass cut for the first time, the heart-lifting smell bringing sudden promise of summer, and then the blackbird, black as the blackest thing in the world, sleek and glossy, banana-yellow beak, moving purposefully about the lawn, fishing for worms. Look closely: observe the yellow ring around the eye as well.

Blackbirds are great garden birds: they love the combination of open ground and cover that many gardens provide. They also like the combination of open ground and trees that is so beloved by municipal parks – one of the few birds that does. That is because they like best to feed on the ground:

sometimes hopping, sometimes running, generally in straight lines, with lots of little pauses.

On a lawn, they will look for worms and yank them out, pink and wriggling. They find them by listening and by looking, standing still between hops.

Once it has found a worm, a foraging blackbird is likely to stay in the same place for a while, because when you've found one, you have quite often found several. Blackbirds study the habits of worms as if their lives depended on it; and for the best of reasons.

Blackbirds find human life reasonably agreeable, and adapt well to the greener places that humans live in. But they also do wild pretty well: they are woodland birds that constantly forsake the trees to feed on the ground. They can be noisy as they beak and scrabble about in the leaf-litter; they can often sound like a fairly chunky mammal bashing his way through the undergrowth.

The females are not black birds at all; they are a discreet dead-leaf brown. That apparent injustice works out well for the females: in territorial disputes, males tend to chase other males. And the young males look like females: a good move, since this means older, tougher males won't be stimulated by the sight of a black, yellow-beaked rival and beat up the hapless youngster.

The sight of a male blackbird – a black blackbird – is part of British life. So is the sound, even if you didn't realise it in your conscious mind. The male blackbird is one of the greatest singers you will ever find; if you spent your life listening to birds all over the world you would be hard pressed to find a singer to compare to the blackbird.

The song is relaxed, effortless, flowing: the bird seems to be leaning against the wall with his hands in his pockets as he whistles. Many of the notes are flute-like and clear; but other bits are far more complicated, with growly, scrapey notes that add a disconcertingly modernist touch to an otherwise traditionalist repertoire.

Repertoire is the word all right, for blackbirds love to invent, reinvent, change and develop their songs. They continue to learn new songs through-out their lives, stringing phrase after phrase together in long, winding sentences.

Why so? The experienced older blackbird – that is to say, the blackbird with the most compli-cated collection of songs – is tougher, better able to function as a mate for the right hen, and better able to deal with any intruding rival male; better, in short, as a rearer of chicks. A long, complex song says: "I'm gorgeous, I'm tough, I'm a blackbird's blackbird. I'm the sort of blackbird that becomes an ancestor – and you can't get sexier than that." Hear two males sing at dawn from their opposed song-posts as if they are fighting a duel. Or sit out in the evening in May, preferably with a nice drink, and listen to the blackbirds. Raise your glass and drink to blackbirds, to beauty, to life. Birdwatching doesn't get much better.

3. Wren

The wren is one of the smallest birds in Britain — and possibly the loudest. If it fails to be *quite* the loudest, it's not for lack of effort. Like a pugnacious dwarf, the wren positively shouts at you. It is the shortest bird in Europe, if you take into account its traditional cocked-tail posture. They are astonishingly small: nine centimetres long, 13 centimetres wingspan. They are great skulkers and lurkers, and yet everything about their character, as we perceive it, is strong, feisty, bold and in-your-face.

They adapt to human surroundings pretty well — but then they adapt to just about everything pretty well, except very hard weather. And even this does not defeat them: the survivors will breed in huge numbers when the better weather comes and make good the losses. They are extraordinarily abundant little birds: you can find them on the coast, up in the mountains; in woods and on farmland, parks and gardens. All they insist on is a decent amount of low vegetation. That thing about lowness is important. You hardly ever need to look up for a wren; you almost always have to look down.

Thickets, brambles, clumps, undergrowth, tangles, and man-made stuff like hedges and shrubberies too. They are fond of the shady places behind sheds and greenhouses. They like it thick and dense, and because they are so ridiculously small, wrens can squeeze in and make a living where other birds are disbarred because of their size. Wrens are just about the best exploiters of the smallness niche in Britain.

They are not all that easy to see, so perhaps you think it was mean of me to put them in the book so early, before you've really warmed up. But they are among the first birds you learn once you begin to use your eyes and ears a bit more effectively. That's mostly because they are everywhere. Think small, think low, think dense, and you have found your wren. And think loud. An outburst, a positive explosion of song from about knee height in a

Wren

Where to look: *tangled undergrowth, low down*
When to look: *all year*
What to look for: *tiny, tawny bird, cocky tail*
What to listen for: *astonishing volume*

hedge: you've found a wren. How does so small a bird make such a racket? By putting absolutely everything into it, its whole body literally quivering with effort.

Just about every outburst ends in a trill – prolonged and incredibly emphatic. A wren may be a lurker, but it is not the least bit shy. A male wren is likely to sing at any time in the year – not as consistently as a robin, but any nice sunny day in autumn and winter will encourage a roaring, cacophonous trill-ending song.

A wren is not a great deal to look at, but what there is is full of character: bright eye picked out by a strong, pale eye-stripe; unmistakable cocky tail. A wren feeding is creeping, mouse-like, making its living by sneaking about in thickets after insects, especially beetles, and they are also keen on spiders. Their main tool is a relatively long beak: they will turn over leaves and stones in a busy, restless search for enough little beasts to fill their tiny but highly demanding stomachs.

Wrens are also capable of explosive ticking sounds. Before I learned the call – all you really have to do here is learn the volume – I remember searching a decent-sized copse that was filled with this huge sound. I thought I had to be onto something pretty big and seriously impressive. It was some time before I discovered that it was something extremely small and very impressive indeed. And they can be pugnacious birds, to other wrens and to other small birds: you'd fancy them to pick a fight with anything. They are wonderfully indomitable – adaptable, clamorous, vehement – tiny birds with a quite colossal presence.

Chaffinch
Where to look: *low branches,*
beneath bird-feeders
When to look: *all year*
What to look for: *blue hat, double*
white wing bar
What to listen for: *finch!*

4. Chaffinch

If chaffinches were rare they would be prized above Siberian rubythroats and red-flanked bluetails. The cock chaffinch in spring is as stunning a little bird as you can see anywhere in the world; and you can see him more or less any time you want to.

They are common birds. That sounds rather disparaging, I know. Actually, the chaffinch's commonness is a tribute to its knack of fitting in to a lot of different circumstances. It should be prized for its commonness, not reviled for it.

The cock is outrageous. Admire him: a cap of more or less Wedgwood blue, conker-brown back, and a breast of the tartiest pink any designer could come up with. The male spring bird is the sexiest thing on two legs, and he is not bashful about it, either.

In winter the males have the same colour scheme, but in much better taste: muted, subtle, colour-coordinated, a bird you could introduce anywhere. The young and the females are much quieter: roughly speaking, a monochrome version of the for-God's-sake-look-at-me male. The easiest way to recognise them is if they are standing next to a male.

But all chaffinches give themselves away in flight. One of the great things you learn, the more you birdwatch, is how to recognise birds from bad sightings. Chaffinches are great birds to train you in that art, because they look so distinctive when they are flying away from you.

From the back, feeding on the ground, when not in clear view, the birds, even the males, can look quite a lot like any other little bird. But when they fly, they explode into a black and white pattern – not exactly black and white, but the white bits stand out quite startlingly from the drabber background colour. Look for two bars on the wing: a big white patch on, if you like, the shoulder, and a second stripe lower down. The outer tail feathers are white as well. They are very nice birds to get the hang of. They do their best to make it easy for you and they should be respected for that, I think.

They are finches, different from the birds we have met already. They are called finches because the chaffinch has a bright cheery call that sounds like "Finch! Finch!" The song, which you are only likely to hear in spring, is loud and distinctive – gathering pace and reaching a neat little climax. Some say that it sounds like a fast bowler's run-up and delivery stride.

Look at the bill. It is noticeably different from the bill of a robin or a wren, which is slim and delicate. Compared to those, a chaffinch's beak – any finch's beak – looks like a pair of nut-crackers, and for the best of reasons. A finch's speciality is seeds; and it opens them with a stout bill, a strong tongue and powerful jaw muscles.

Beaks are things to pay attention to. As we move on through the book, we will see more and more different kinds of beaks: spears, meat-hooks, fish-gaffes, chisels, lawnmowers, razors, tweezers and cleavers. The beak is made from stuff called keratin, which is also found in the skin of mammals (like ourselves). Beaks, claws and feathers all use keratin. It is wonderfully versatile stuff, and the forces of evolution can mould it like putty. The fine little probe of a robin's beak and the ludicrous Dutch clog of a shoebill's bill are made of the same stuff and shaped by the same forces.

And the finch's beak is a perfect example of the versatility of keratin, of beaks, of birds. A beak is the bird's hand, if you like, and a toolkit as well: a crucial part of how it makes its way in the world.

Finches have their nutcrackers, and that is something that frees them from the difficult task of finding insects in hard weather. They eat invertebrates in the spring and the summer – juicy green caterpillars when they can get them – and they mostly feed in trees; but when it gets colder, they look for seeds on the ground. Their tough little beaks enable them to reach the hefty chunk of protein you find inside a seedcase.

You can find chaffinches on the ground by bird-feeders: they don't have the acrobatic habit and inclination to use them properly, but they are not averse to picking up scraps released by the scramblers and climbers. They are common because they are effective and adaptable birds; and there is no prettier bird than a chaffinch in this, or any other, bird-book: common birds with a rare beauty.

5. Thrush

Well, there are five thrushes that you can see regularly in this country: that is to say, five birds whose scientific name amusingly begins with the word Turdus. We have already dealt with one, in fact – the blackbird is *Turdus merula*.

But we generally think of thrushes as the browny, speckly-breasted birds we see hopping about on the grass. There are two of these on the likely-to-see list: mistle thrush and song thrush. And the one you are more likely to see in a garden is song thrush. If it flies high to the treetops, it's a mistle, if it flits away to the nearest hedge, it's a song. The song thrush is smaller, and appreciates good cover. If you see a bird feeding in loads of open space, like the middle of a playing-field, it is probably a mistle thrush. If it is under a bush in your garden, it is more likely to be a song thrush.

The mistle thrush is big, chunky, and hops in a bold, rather in-your-face way. The song thrush gives an altogether less obstreperous vibe. In wildish places, like countryside and woodland, they are not terribly easy to see; but in gardens, they can be almost as trusting as robins, though without the robin's apparent matiness.

They eat mainly small invertebrates, worms especially, and are famously talented as escargot gourmets: they will catch snails and then get rid of the shells by bashing them against a stone. Thrushes have favourite anvil stones for this tricky task, and will return to them again and again. They are the only British bird that does this, so if you see a bird beating a snail to death, you don't have to spend hours thumbing through your field guide to get an identification. You might hear it in action first – a curiously slapping, lip-smacking sound.

Thrushes also take fruit and berries when they are available; you can often see them pecking at windfalls beneath apple trees, and if you put some bits of fruit out beneath – rather than on – your bird-table, you have every chance of getting a visit from a song thrush.

Song thrush
Where to look: *lawns, ground near cover*
When to look: *all year*
What to look for: *speckled breast*
What to listen for: *repeating song in spring, smack of snail against stone*

But why are they called song thrushes? All thrushes sing – what is so special about the song of the song thrush? The song thrush has a truly exceptional talent. It is wonderfully loud. It is also an extremely easy song to get the hang of. A song thrush loves, above all things, repetition. So if, in spring, you hear a bird that sings the same loud, ringing phrase, and then repeats it two or three times, you have a song thrush. Browning got it right:

> That's the wise thrush; he sings each song twice over,
> Lest you think he never could recapture
> The first fine careless rapture!

They will pick a phrase, sometimes sweet and fluty, sometimes big and operatic, sometimes harsh, grating and more challenging. And they will then give it to you again. Sometimes, if they especially like it, they will let it rip four or five times.

The phrases have any number of variations and thrushes also love to mimic. They aren't, generally, precise mimics: they take an original idea and turn it into a song of their own. They are the jazz musicians of suburbia. They mimic other birds, of course, but often, they will bring non-bird sounds into their repeating improvisations. Occasionally they can be found imitating Trimphones, the warbling "modernistic" telephone of the 60s. I have heard recordings of a song thrush imitating a shepherd whistling to his dog, and of another imitating a lawnmower. Thrushes are inventive and experimental musicians, and the more inventive they are, the sexier they are.

I'd better run through the other obvious thrushes while we are here. The mistle thrush, chunkier as I say, tends to fly high; a song thrush generally flies lower. A mistle thrush has very noticeable white underwings – white armpits if you prefer. Mistle thrushes are fearless birds, and when their nest is threatened by a magpie, they will charge at him with mad football-rattle threat-calls. Their song, often described as "wild and skirling" is a special joy because it comes so early in the year: they are real harbingers of spring.

The blackbird we have already dealt with. The other two species of Turdus are generally seen in the winter, coming to us from further north. British winters are something we complain about, but they are balmy for a bird that summers in Scandinavia. You can see fieldfares in big flocks in open fields: they have black tails and make a pleasing triple-cluck as they fly by. Redwings also like open spaces and go about in flocks. They are a good brick-red colour just below the wing when it is closed, but the red extends up to the armpit when they fly. They also have a distinctive eyebrow, and are more striped than spotted underneath.

The song thrush is, apart from the blackbird, the most easy thrush to see. And that song – I implore you to listen for that song.

City

6. Sparrow

The bird of the city: that's the sparrow. It's not proper – perhaps it's not even legal – to have a city without sparrows. That's true not just in this country, but all over the world. Dr Dolittle's sparrow friend, a committed urbanite, was called Cheapside. A Londoner may be affectionately referred to as a "real cockney sparrer". The name of sparrow conjures up the idea of something perky, indomitable, uncrushable: a cheerful and inevitable part of daily life. "Common as sparrows" we say; the very idea of commonness is embodied in the name of sparrow.

The house sparrow, that is, of course; not Britain's other sparrow, the elusive tree sparrow,

House Sparrow

Where to look: *roofs, hedges*
When to look: *all year*
What to look for: *black beard*
What to listen for: *cheep-cheep*

these days a worryingly scarce country bumpkin.

The male house sparrow is strongly handsome, or would be considered so if sparrows were less familiar – nicely put together in tasteful shades of brown, black and grey, with that little chain of white along the upper wing. The female is very different – much more restrained and demure in colouring.

But the thing about the sparrow is that they are no longer as common as sparrows. In 1925, a count of birds in Kensington Gardens included 2,600 house sparrows. Seventy-five years later, another count found just eight – a decline of 99.7 per cent.

The gap between these two counts covers a gradual, long-term decline, and a more recent and more sudden falling-off. In horse-drawn London, the sparrows could find food everywhere, in spilt grain and in droppings. As the working horse became extinct in London, so the sparrows declined. But there was still a hefty population: wherever humans lived in houses, there were sparrows about the place. Loads of them.

But they have fallen away again, and this time no one is quite sure why. The decline has been going on since the 80s. Before that, there is not much evidence to go on. Why bother to study the population of sparrows, when there were so many? Sparrows were just too common to bother with. Since then, some closely observed populations have declined by 80 per cent.

Loss of food, especially of the highly nutritious aphids that they feed to their young; loss of nesting sites; increased numbers of predators (especially the domestic cat); competition for food; disease: all these things have been suggested. One possibility is that the changes in agriculture have affected even the town populations; the vast winter flocks of sparrows over open fields are no longer seen. There is no longer so much grain spilt about the place.

All this means that the house sparrow cannot now be taken for granted. And, as a result, we feel that little bit more privileged when we clap eyes on one. At bird tables, they are no longer to be regarded as an irritation – stealing food from the prettier birds we had been hoping to attract. These days, sparrows need to be enjoyed for their own sake.

These birds have put up with just about everything that humans can throw at them, including the pollution and the pea-soupers of Victorian London, and the Blitz. They are highly effective survivors, and they have a splendid affinity for us humans.

Sparrows have the most tremendous gift for adaptability. Adaptability is the key for all birds that have managed to live in cities alongside humans.

Most birds can't do it. They find themselves stuck in the tender trap of specialisation: perfectly evolved for a way of life that has been taken from them. You won't find a woodpecker making a go of city life, or a diving duck. But sparrows have a very appealing resourcefulness. Away from humans, they live mostly on plant material: shoots, buds, berries and so forth. But those that have moved into human settlements also thrive on bread, cooked potatoes, meat; and anything they can steal from domestic animals. It is easy to imagine that the very first human settlements in the country had sparrows chirping around the animals, and the rubbish tips and the food stores, nesting in the grass thatch, and soothing the inhabitants with their chirpiness.

Sparrows like company, noise and bustle. Even in their private lives they seem always to have been city birds – waiting through their evolutionary history for the moment when the cities were invented, so that they could unleash their full potential. They like to be in flocks, where they can cheep at each other, quarrel and compete.

The news that house sparrows are so much rarer does at least mean we can appreciate them a little more. But there is also a solemn lesson to be learned here: that nothing in the natural world can be taken for granted, and that survival is not guaranteed. This is a fragile world we live in, and when we think of the scruffy, swaggering, self-confident, never-give-up, always-about nature of the house sparrow and learn about its sudden, unthought-of and catastrophic problems, it is time for us to get better at the art of cherishing.

7. Pigeon

Look up pigeon in your good field guide, if you have one. You will probably find that the pigeon does not exist. The most obvious bird in the country doesn't even rate a mention. There seems to be a conspiracy of silence about the pigeon, as if pigeons were an embarrassment to birdwatchers – as if pigeons were an embarrassment to proper birds.

Pigeons, however, exist. There they are, eating McDonald's chips at railway stations, hanging about on precipitous ledges above the hooting streets, pursuing their love lives with unbridled enthusiasm around the ankles of pedestrians. Try telling them they are not proper birds.

In most good field guides, you will, if you look,

find a brief mention of the city pigeon under rock dove. You will find a rather grudging admission that feral forms of this otherwise nice bird exist, and are highly variable. The variation itself seems to give offence to the writers of good field guides.

The city pigeon, then, is a rock dove that has gone funny. The rock dove, in its pure form, can be found in western Ireland and northern and western Scotland. It likes ledges and high places. Perhaps that sounds familiar. And, surprisingly, the rock dove, it was discovered, has a great affinity for human beings.

Pigeons are easily domesticated, breeding well and confidently. They have been bred for meat for thousands of years. They have been bred for all sorts of other reasons; mostly, I suspect, because humans just like to breed them. They can be bred like dogs – different sizes and shapes and colours, but all the same species. In fact, Charles Darwin spent years breeding domestic pigeons himself. He wanted to understand the way they vary, according to the way you breed them. This was an absolutely vital part of his preparation for the book that changed our understanding of the world: *On the Origin of Species*.

Pigeons also have an extraordinary ability to return to the place they live. They have a strange sensitivity to the earth's magnetic field. This is all the more intriguing because the pigeon is not a species

Wood Pigeon

Where to look: *high trees, flocks in open fields*
When to look: *all year*
What to look for: *white neck-patches*
What to listen for: *steal twoooo cows, Taffy*

that goes in for long-distance migrations. However, this ability has meant that pigeons have been bred to carry messages, or to race. You often see a small group of pigeons in a loose gathering of a dozen or so, flying without undue hurry but with great confidence and purpose. These are probably racers, making the long way home to the loft.

Domestic pigeons have, inevitably, escaped, and bred – and found that the high ledges of the cities were just as good for them as cliffs: church steeples and towers, public offices, museums, railway stations, factories, warehouses, gabled houses, turrets, cupolas, angled rain-pipes, ventilators, airbrick spaces, eaves, lofts and attics. They learned to use a city's food resources as well: bread, biscuits, peanuts, banana, apple peel, potato, cheese, fish, meat, fat, chocolate, ice-cream. And so they prospered and spread, and did so in a multitude of forms: some like the ancestral rock doves, others in all manner of fancy colours, some sleek and beautiful, others wacky and clownish. Sometimes, these outlandish forms breed back to the pure rock dove form.

The reward for all this is to be called a pest. The word "pest" means any living thing that is inconvenient to humans, as if only one species had a right to this planet, and all the rest were here on sufferance. I don't wish to pursue this argument to the logical extreme, but I find feral pigeons cheering and diverting members of the community, and worth tolerating a few smelly places for. A few dribbles of whitewash along a building indicate life to me, not a dreadful evidence of shame and neglect.

Most of the information you find about feral pigeons is about how to kill them. "Out of control" is the big scary line you keep running across – as if it was essential for all untamed animals to be under human control. I am not advocating the spreading of disease by any means, but I don't subscribe to the universal hate-the-pigeon campaign. Pigeons are clever; they come in different colours and forms; they are messy; they are noisy; and they are very, very determined to survive. Just like humans, really. No wonder we hate them.

But there's more to pigeons than just the city variety. There are two other species that we must consider before moving on, even if they are not city birds. The first is the wood pigeon – quite different from the rock dove/feral pigeon/domestic pigeon/city pigeon. Wood pigeons wouldn't dream of interbreeding with them; and that's the big test.

Wood pigeons are not such relentless urbanites. They need big trees; they are good at parks and gardens and countryside. They are easy enough to identify: big, with a very clear white patch on each side of the neck and the bold white patch on the wing. In the countryside in winter, you see them in strikingly big gatherings. In the spring you hear them all the time: a complicated cooing. Apologies to sensitive Celts here, but this old story is the best way to remember the call – advice from a pigeon to a Welshman who has stolen a cow: "Steal twoooo cows, Taffy." If you flush a bird from cover, and hear a great wing-clapping, twig-breaking explosion of sound, you have disturbed a wood pigeon.

The other pigeon-relative you are likely to see is the collared dove: a bird that has become common among us in a shockingly short space of time, spreading from the south through entirely natural means. The collared dove is a very pretty, pinky-grey bird with a thick black half-collar. The tail is very white at the tip, and very obvious, as the bird tends to flirt its tail extravagantly on landing, often making a triumphant gargling call, celebrating the fact. In spring, it makes a monotonous triple-coo that reminds some observers of a football fan, chanting dismally: "Un-i-ted! Un-i-ted!" They are lovely birds to see, far more delicate than the wood pigeon or the unmentionable city pigeon. They are especially comely in flight, where they can look like a small flock of angels. They are a reminder that nothing in wildlife is settled, and that not all changes are for the worse.

8. Starling

Starlings are the most spectacular birds in Britain. Certainly, they provide the most extraordinary spectacle that any British bird is capable of putting on. Perhaps that seems an extreme claim for one of the more humdrum birds, but no one who has seen starlings in the winter dusk could disagree.

Starlings are sociable birds. They like to form loose flocks, even in the breeding season, a time when most birds are eager to be half of a pair and to leave it at that. But in the winter, starlings take their sociability to an almost human level. They like to share an evening roost. A place with plenty of perching room becomes a hugely attractive thing for more and more starlings.

Starling
Where to look: *anywhere*
When to look: *all year, big flocks in winter*
What to look for: *dark bird with speckles, paler and more speckly in winter*
What to listen for: *clicks, wheezes, imitations*

And just before it is time for them to sleep for the night, they will take to the air and fly. Fly in huge dense crowds, frequently of up to 100,000, and sometimes of a million and more birds. They make a huge, oozing, seething mass, changing shape and direction, now like smoke, now like a cloud, now like an aerial river, now like a whirlpool. It is enthralling and dizzying to see them, and the wild rustle of their wings as they pass overhead is a sound of astonishing volume.

Why do they do it? How do they know what to do? How come they don't keep bumping into each other? It is a sight that amazes me, every time, and I have seen ornithological wonders all over the world. It seems to be a kind of celebration, a celebration of togetherness, a consolidation of the flock, a sort of bonding session, in which each bird flies to establish, maintain, and strengthen the idea that every individual starling is at his best when one of many. That's how it looks to me, anyway.

Starlings are spectacular in other ways, too. They are the best mimics of all the British birds – more accurate than the song thrush already mentioned, and more various. Individuals will have 15 or 20 different sounds that they can mimic; sounds they mix up with the starling's habitual repertoire of clucks, wheezes and whistles. The starling is an astonishing virtuoso.

A friend of mine who was a warden for the RSPB told me he knew that there were black-tailed godwits breeding on his reserve as soon as he heard starlings making black-tailed godwit breeding-calls. Starlings are especially fond of buzzard and chicken impersonations, and they will also happily do goats, frogs, cats and humans.

All of which is impressive for a much overlooked bird. Starlings are blackish at a distance but, close up, the adult birds are a deep iridescent purple, lavishly spangled and speckled. In winter, the speckles are bigger and almost cover the face and throat with frosty white. They are a little smaller than a blackbird, with a thin, sharp beak and a flat head. They are birds of cities, certainly, but they are also birds of the suburbs, of parks and of the countryside. They are, like all city birds, wonderfully various in their habits and their diets.

Starlings are especially fond of small invertebrates, insects and spiders, and the way they gather these is a tribute to their genius for reinventing themselves. As starlings mimic a dozen birds by sound, so they seem to mimic a dozen birds in their foraging techniques. You will sometimes see starlings hunting through the fur of domestic animals, like the oxpeckers of Africa (a reasonably close relation) do with wild buffalo. They will forage in the trees, like finches. They will rifle through vegetation on the ground, and they will probe the earth with their beaks, like blackbirds and thrushes. They have extra-strong muscles that allow them to open their beaks once inserted in the ground, a highly useful trick. They can also swivel their eyes to watch for danger from behind; they will sometimes hang from bird-feeders, like tits, and will even hawk for insects on the wing, like swallows. It seems that there is no end to their talents.

Look for starlings in flocks of any size, from half a dozen to a million – each bird making a characteristic triangular silhouette. On the ground – again, generally in a group – they will tend to walk rather than hop. In flight they always look rushed, and seem to come into the landing just a shade too fast. They are noisy, and a touch quarrelsome. But quarrelling is for the starling just another vitally important aspect of their lives of intense togetherness.

Bird-feeder

9. Blue tit

As millennium followed millennium, as the world changed along with the vegetation and the climate upon it, as the Darwinian forces shaped the living creatures to suit the changing world, so the blue tit was driven by these inexorable forces into startling and complete perfection, a bird evolved for taking advantage of the bird-feeders in British gardens.

The invention of the bird-feeder has made the blue tit the star of the garden: the acrobat, charmer, crowd-pleaser, the feathered genius. The packing of peanuts in a mesh tube gives the blue tit a matchless opportunity to do what it does best – hang upside down and forage, and to do so with wit, skill, precision and daring.

Blue Tit

Where to look: *bird-feeders, trees*
When to look: *all year*
What to look for: *yellow breast, blue cap*
What to listen for: *churrr*

Blue tits have always been great favourites, because they are colourful and small and bold. But the bird-feeder has brought them centre stage. Blue tits have always been pushy and canny, and are always ready to take advantage of a food source, even if it comes in an unfamiliar form. They have evolved to be acrobatic. They have also evolved to be self-confident, inquisitive and capable of exploiting unexpected opportunities.

It was the blue tits who first realised that doorstep milk-bottles contained valuable food: and it was the blue tits who learned how to peck them open and drink the cream from the top. Was this the intuitive brilliance of a single avian Einstein? How was it that this skill became part of blue tit culture in an almost instantaneous flash of time? These matters are to be numbered among the eternal mysteries of life. The blue tit's eureka moment was later picked up by many other birds, but it was the blue tits that showed the way. They are, by nature, pioneers.

But it was not, of course, for bird-feeders that they evolved their matchless acrobatic skills and their curiosity. They are a bird of deciduous woodland, and they forage for food on the extreme edges of trees: at the end of the twigs. Their skills at acrobatics opened food resources for them that were unavailable to less adroit birds.

On the feeder, they will get hooshed off by the great tits, who are much bigger and bolder. Great tits have a bright yellow breast with a black stripe down it, a bright white cheek on a glossy black head. They too are good at using the feeder. They are not as agile as the blue tits, being bigger and more cumbersome, but they get more time, because a blue tit can't hoosh a great tit off. The two species don't clash when they return to the trees. They both like the same sort of trees, but the great tit specialises in the middle parts while the blue tit prefers the edges. Their different sizes, their different natures, make for a highly workable system.

The great tit is a far more strident singer. As the spring begins to take hold and the first fine days of the year begin to establish themselves, so the great tit will start to sing "teacher, teacher": loud and strongly disyllabic. The first great tit of the spring is always one of the year's better moments. Great tits have a huge range and variation: one of the standard rules of birdwatching is if you hear a call you have never heard in your life before, it's a great tit.

There is a third tit that will come to the bird-feeder: smaller even than the blue tit, and with a white badger stripe on the back of its neck. This is the coal tit, and even the blue tit can hoosh him off the peanuts. Accordingly, he spends little time there; he holds to the policy of grab a nut and go. Away from the feeder, the coal tit forages for tiny insects in between the needles of pine trees, and his acrobatics can even make a blue tit look clumsy. Being the right size is one of the crucial skills in life.

There is one more tit I must tell you about. This is a bird that many casual birdwatchers never see, and yet once you have got the key, it is amazingly common. In the cooler months especially, the long-tailed tit is a constant delight. Listen for the triple-squeak, a thin "sisisi", uttered by one bird, and another and another and another – and then sometimes an abrupt stutter. When you see a long-tailed tit, you tend to see a lot of them, going around in gangs of a dozen or more, generally in the high part of trees.

They will cross from tree to tree – two, three, or more in a line astern – always "sisisi"-ing to each other to keep together as they forage. They are tiny, and make an unmistakable stick-and-ball shape when they fly. If you ever see a tiny bird with far more than its fair share of tail, and accompanied by a lot of others just the same, you are looking at long-tailed tits. They will come to the feeders sometimes, and will also forage on the ground beneath. And they, too, are highly acrobatic.

The tits are delightful birds; they have colour and style and sparkiness. They have evolved in a way that is, quite by chance, so pleasing to us humans that we put out special food for them. You can't help feeling that this is one of the most brilliant evolutionary stratagems of all time. I wish that every bird was so greatly cherished by human beings; I wish we could provide for the needs of every bird.

But the blue tit has special role to play: a sort of public relations man for the rest of aviankind; a bird that is easy to see, and easy to enjoy, and easy to cherish. The blue tits provide a kind of gateway into caring about wildlife: they show us what we humans can do for birds, if we can be bothered. And blue tits have the added charm of looking grateful for it. The blue tits delight us; but, canniest of all, they flatter us. Smart little birds.

Greenfinch
Where to look: *bird-feeders, trees*
When to look: *all year*
What to look for: *yellow flash on wings, easily visible even when closed*
What to listen for: *zweeee in spring*

10. Greenfinch

Greenfinches are probably the worst bird-feeder birds you will see. They really are pretty hopeless; they look about as at home hanging sideways off a feeder as an eagle. It's not what they're built for; they are not supposed to be acrobatic and nimble and clever. But they are no fools: they see a decent food resource and they abandon dignity like a shot and go for it with everything they have. That is what survival is all about. It is better to admire them for their adaptable minds than to mock them for their dodgy technique on the trapeze.

They are handsome birds – plump-looking and chunky, with a large beak and a noticeably forked tail. The drawback is that they don't look terribly green. Only when you catch them in strong sun-light do you say, "Ah yes, they really are rather green, those finches."

In sombre light they are a collection of mossy, olivey greens. But they have two very distinct give-aways: a yellow flash on the wings, prominent even when the wings are folded, and the same colour tastefully echoed on the outer tail feathers, most obvious as they fly away.

They are seed-eaters – that is what the hefty bill is all about. They are crackers and munchers of seeds – their beaks are powerful and effective and that, along with their enquiring nature, is what enables them to adapt to many different kinds of seed. This is a package that has allowed them to prosper when so many other birds have declined. Adaptability is a great source of strength, especially in a world that is being rapidly changed by humans.

You will find greenfinches just about anywhere where there are tall trees, open sunny places and access to the ground. Gardens, parks, orchards, even graveyards: greenfinches have spread out well beyond their traditional edge-of-woodland habitat.

Greenfinches are seriously dedicated to seeds; they will take the seeds from a fruit and leave the flesh. They will also go through the droppings of members of the thrush family. Thrushes like flesh but not seeds, and, if any get ingested by mistake, they will tend to pass them through unscathed. So a greenfinch will help himself to thrush droppings, which is no doubt why thrushes have the generic name of Turdus.

In fact, greenfinches will take seeds from all sort of unlikely sources. Few other birds will take rose-hips, but greenfinches will. They are also very keen on the seeds of yew trees, and there is not much competition for them, either. The rapid spread of greenfinches through human parks and gardens over recent decades has been put down to their taste for the seeds of spurge laurel.

You tend to see greenfinches most often in winter. In the harder months of the year, they tend to hang around in flocks, and will make foraging raids on bird-feeders in groups of half a dozen or so. They are cheerful, busy, preoccupied birds.

In the spring they are easier to hear than to see. Their song sounds almost like somebody's impersonation of birdsong: a series of thoughtful, richly produced trills, the best of them really quite striking. They also make a sound that is quite unmistakable once you have got the hang of it: a buzzy, rather sleepy, slurred sort of "zweeeeee". That "zweeeeee" is one of the sounds of spring, and once you have got it, you will always have greenfinches with you.

11. Nuthatch

It really is quite easy to identify a nuthatch. They have their heads at the bottom of their bodies and their bums at the top. And if that is an exaggeration, it is only a slight one. No bird is as happy upside down as a nuthatch. Its preferred position in life is on a stout tree trunk with its head pointing at the ground and its tail turned up to the leaves above.

The tits that come to the nut-feeder are wonderfully acrobatic, but you never get the idea that their hearts and souls are upside down. The nuthatch lives for being upside down; it lives in a world in which the trees hang downwards from a ceiling of grass and there is a floor of blue miles and miles below.

Nuthatch

Where to look: *bird-feeders, high, mature trees*
When to look: *all year*
What to look for: *upside-down bird with black eyeliner*
What to listen for: *referee's whistle*

Nuthatches will come to a bird-feeder in a determinedly upside down mood. They will perch on the feeder, bums to the sky, and bash and tease out the nuts with their heads downward – not hanging off, like a tit, but perched full square on the feeder, head-down and chipping away.

They are striking birds, slatey-blue above, buff underneath, with chestnut sides, and the exotic touch of a load of black eyeliner. This thick black eye-stripe gives a distinctly stylish air to the birds, even if they do look a bit like 1920s vamps who have overdone the kohl.

Nuthatches are tree-lovers above all, and they are pretty precise about the kind of trees they like. They won't come to everybody's feeder, and have only recently spread as far north as Scotland. You need the right kind of trees if you are to get nuthatches. But if there are the right kind of trees nearby – big oaks, hornbeam, and especially beeches – then chances are that you will get nuthatches on the feeder.

When nuthatches aren't upside down eating your peanuts, they are upside down on the trunks and branches of trees, looking for small beasts, insects and other invertebrates and, in winter, seeds. They like their trees to be big and mature, with fat trunks and stout branches and hefty twig clusters.

You don't often get trees like this in over-managed forest, where they take out trees when they reach a certain size. But in open woodland, groves and parkland, you get plenty of nuthatch trees, and therefore plenty of nuthatches.

That beak is the thing to look for: a short spear, sharply pointed, and capable of being used with force and precision through the mesh of a feeder or in the cracks of bark. The beak is a probe and a stabber, not often used as a chisel, like a wood-pecker's.

They are anti-social birds, even as nestlings. They like to set up a territory and hold it through-out the year, like a robin, and do so mainly as half of a pair. They are tough customers at the feeder, and can see off any tit species. Being bigger than great tits and much more formidably armed, it hardly ever comes to a fight. A wing-riffle and a piercing Paddington Bear stare is normally enough to make sure that the nuthatch has the feeder to himself.

They are very vocal birds, with a wide range of whistles: simple and uncomplicated and often very sweet. Song thrush, in particular, love to incorpo-rate nuthatch sounds into their repertoire. But a nuthatch won't get bored with his whistle and change theme, as a thrush will. If you hear a sound like a referee's whistle, endlessly repeated, you are listening to a nuthatch.

It is hard to see them when they are doing their natural stuff on a tree trunk; bringing them in close is one of the great jobs that a feeder does for you. On trees, they generally forage upside down, heading downwards, but they are by no means dogmatic about this. They are erratic, and change course frequently when tempted by a promising-looking bit of branch.

Nuthatches are the only birds you will see that are capable of moving head first down a tree trunk. Other birds will invert, but only a nuthatch habitually prefers to live its life the wrong way up.

Sky

12. Swallow

My old friend, the late Dylan Aspinwall, was one of the great pioneers of ornithology in Zambia. He was the prime mover of the Zambian bird atlas project, for which I did a tiny bit of work on a couple of occasions, in the company, needless to add, of a very good birdwatcher indeed. Dylan relished a joke, and would even put jokes into high and serious books of ornithology. He co-authored an essential book for Zambian birdwatching, with the unforgettable title: *A Field Guide to Zambian Birds Not Found In Southern Africa*. I am absolutely certain that Dylan himself was solely responsible for the books' brief guide to habitat. It begins, under the heading *"Sky"*, with the words:

Swallow

Where to look: *sky, telegraph wires*
When to look: *mid-spring to early autumn*
What to look for: *tail-streamers, belly-scraping ground-attack*
What to listen for: *two-note swit-wit when flying into the outbuilding where it has built its nest*

"The sky is the most widespread habitat in Zambia."

By one of those amazing coincidences, the sky is almost equally widespread in this country. And just like Zambian skies, it is a habitat for birds. Why is the sky a habitat for birds? Because there is food for birds to be found in it: insects, spiders, and other flying, floating and drifting edible beasts, that are collectively known as "aerial plankton". Where there is a food source, it is a fair bet that some creature or other will discover a way of exploiting it.

But now hear something truly amazing. One of the most widespread inhabitants of the widespread Zambian sky is also one of the most widespread inhabitants of the widespread British skies. It is the same species, and it is the swallow. Zambian bird-watchers will tell you that the swallow – they will call it European swallow to distinguish it from a number of other kinds – is an African bird that chooses to breed in Europe.

We think of the swallow as a quintessentially English, or British bird, and associate it with low skimming flight across cricket fields as the last overs are played out. Cricketers move on, feeling the need to discuss proceedings in the gardens of pubs, drinking warm beer, in the warm evening, while swallows criss-cross the sky above them until it gets dark.

Where do swallows go in the winter? This was once one of the great mysteries of the world. Gilbert White, the 18th-century parson who more or less invented birdwatching, pondered the matter time and again in his famous *Chronicles of Selborne*. Did they fly somewhere else? Or did they bury themselves in the mud at the bottom of ponds and hibernate?

We know now, of course. And the swallow is one of the most important birds in the British year. More than any other birds, swallows are considered the first sign of spring: one swallow doesn't make a summer, we are warned, but on the other hand, see one swallow and it's a pretty fair bet that the rest of them won't be far behind. They seem to come to England towing the warm weather behind them – blessed birds who bring hope and light back into our lives.

They are most often seen in the air; skilled aerobats, natty in navy on the top and pale below, with a rusty-red patch on the throat that shows up well when you get a good view. But admire the shape rather than the colour: the slim, swept-back wings, the tapering, forked tail, the slender, pared-down silhouette – things that give swallows both speed and manoeuverability. A fighter pilot requires the same attributes from his aircraft; that is why fighter planes have a swept-back swallow silhouette. The song, though, is hardly warlike – a pretty, rather jumbled twittering,

Despite their lofty, unearthly life, swallows are very keen on their association with humans beings, loving to hunt over open land that humans have created, and preferring to build their nests in places humans have built: sheds, barns (Americans call the same species "barn swallows"), stables, garages and car ports – building a mud cup, preferably tucking neatly onto a beam, to get a little support from below. They get more and more sociable as the autumn comes upon us, gathering in long groups on telegraph wires, where they look like notes of music. They are preparing for the impossible journey back south to Africa.

Swallows are closely related to house martins, birds that also live the aerial life. The two species are easy enough to tell apart: house martins are also navy on top and pale below, but they have unmissible white bums. Where swallows twitter, martins blow merry raspberries to each other. Martins like to nest on the sides of houses, beneath the eaves, preferably in a small colony.

Martins, on the whole, prefer the suburbs of towns, while the swallows are more often seen in open countryside – but that's just a generalisation.

I live ten miles from the nearest town and one glorious day every April, I cheer at the return of the martins, spinning round the house, blowing their raspberries, checking out last year's nests to see how much repair work is needed for next year.

The house has been there for half a millennium. It is probable that the martins that nest under its eaves can trace their pedigree back to those martins that first decided that this house was a decent spot to spend a summer, and raise a family.

House martin
Where to look: *nests under the eaves of houses*
When to look: *late spring, summer*
What to look for: *white bums*
What to listen for: *airborne raspberries*

13. Swift

We are drawn to birds because, above all else, they can fly. Our hearts take wing at the sight of a soaring bird. However, all other birds are but amateurs in the art of flight when it comes to the swifts. Swifts are so much masters of the sky that the ground has become a no-go area for them.

They come late in the spring, and they leave early. They are here between May and mid-August: one hot mid summer day you suddenly realise that it is a few days since you last saw a swift. Even at its height, the summer is gone.

They are not so very much like swallows once you look at them – no, not even that closely related. Their body plan is similar, but swifts are far more profoundly committed to the habitat of the sky. Their wings make an easy curve, like a scythe; and often, you will see them very high indeed. They are at home at the dizziest heights, and they will ascend and descend to whatever level they find their aerial plankton.

If you see a bird perched, it is not a swift. Swifts don't. They can cling to a vertical surface, but their undercarriage has been drastically reduced because of their commitment to the air. How committed is that? When a young swift leaves its nest, it could be the last time it touches down for the next two years. Or even three.

Two years of unbroken flight. They feed on the wing, sleep on the wing, fly from Europe to Africa, fly above Africa eating and sleeping, fly back to Europe. As non-breeders in the first year, they will merely continue flying. Back again to Africa, back once again to Europe, where they will find a mate and – yes – they will copulate in the sky.

They were cave-nesters originally, but now they like to get under the roofs of buildings and nest in colonies in these man-made caves. This adaptability has certainly helped them to spread in very decent numbers. And in July and early August, they will give wonderfully mad performances. They love to fly and as they fly, they scream, like customers

Swift

Where to look: *sky*
When to look: *late spring to midsummer*
What to look for: *flying scythe*
What to listen for: *mad screaming*

riding the big dipper – bunches of them hooligan-
ing around the rooftops, along streets, whizzing
round corners on impossible turns, in hair-raising-
ly fast low-level flights, chasing each other; and
always screaming at the tops of their voices. It is the
sound of the early summer, that madcap screaming.
Swifts love company, and they love flight above
everything else, and so they express their flocking
nature in these high-speed, whirling, screaming
crowds.

As for colour, they don't go in for it much: a
dusky brown all over, lighter on the throat, generally looking dark, even black, since they are almost
invariably seen silhouetted against the sky. Watch
the wing-beat, significantly different to the swallow
– very fast, almost shivering wings, held stiffly,
quite different to the bendiness of the swallow's
wing. They will throw in the odd glide from time to
time as well.

Many Mediterranean towns are almost overrun
– certainly overflown – in the summer; the main
squares alive with a screaming of swifts. The birds
provide a splendid cabaret for that finest of
Mediterranean sports – sitting in the main square
and having a drink. They are worth watching
closely. In the harsh Mediterranean light, their
wings will sometimes fizz and glow with light –

an almost hallucinatory effect.

Swifts are the ultimate avian flying machine, and perhaps that makes them the ultimate birds. They have a rare capacity for lifting the heart: with their arrival, scything back into England to send us a sign that the darkness has really gone, and then cheering us throughout their brief stay by their uncanny mastery of the air and by their wild, life-loving careerings.

There is a pub I go to in summer because it is perfect for swift-watching. Perhaps the right word here is swifting. Long evenings of summer are lit up with the scream and dash of swifts – birds worth raising a glass to.

And then they are gone, and if we are sad to lose them, they bring huge cheer to Africans when they arrive. Because of their canny ability to surf along on the weather fronts for their travels, they will often turn up with the rain-clouds, arriving to end the fearsome hot and dry spells that old Africa hands call "the suicide months". Swifts seem to specialise in the art of bringing relief after a bad time.

Swifts are the masters of the air and the habitual conquerors of human misery. If you want to be considered the ultimate bird, that, it seems to me, is not a bad start.

Skylark

Where to look: *sky in spring, otherwise on the ground*
When to look: *all year*
What to look for: *tiny bird above a field on an invisible string*
What to listen for: *endless spring song, the bird never takes a breath*

14. Skylark

The skylark is actually a ground bird. And for most of the year it is invisible: just another small brown bird, with nothing interesting or remarkable about it. For all but a short part of the year, the skylark is one of the most ignored birds in the country. Nobody pays it a second glance.

But in spring, all this changes. At a stroke, this drab little bird turns into the most astonishing and spectacular bird in the world. All at once, it takes to the sky, opens its beak and its heart, and sings. It does more than sing, it fills the air with sound; and those of us on the ground marvel at how so great a wonder can exist and, more prosaically, how it can sing so long and so hard without taking a breath.

The great radio naturalist and author of the Romany books, G. Bramwell Evens, once spoke at the Congregational Hall in Wigan, and my father has never forgotten it. Romany asked: "How many of you could run round the school playing-field?" A forest of hands, naturally. "And how many of you could run round the school playing-field while singing the Hallelujah Chorus?"

Paradoxically, you only find skylarks where there is a lot of ground. Open ground, that is: farm-land and moorland, mainly, though you can find them on sand-dunes, golf courses and yes, school playing-fields. They feed mainly on insects and seeds, as available, and do their foraging on the ground. A skylark spends most of its time with its feet touching the earth; you rarely see it perched anywhere else. It might pause for a moment on a bit of rock or a low bush, but never on a high wire or a tree. Skylarks, when not singing the Hallelujah Chorus, like to be low.

You can pick them out on a walk without too much trouble, as you accidentally flush them from cover. They have noticeably triangular wings with a pale trailing edge, and distinct white outer tail feathers. And that's about as much entertainment as they offer the casual observer for nine or ten months of the year – a bird flying away, very low, with a little flash of white and a low chirrup.

And then the year turns and spring stirs the skylark's blood, and the cock bird is up and singing "Hallelujah". It begins with a silent climb to about 30 metres, and then the rich uninterrupted flow of notes begins. The flight will stabilise at anything from 50 to 100 metres up, and then the bird will circle or, more characteristically, hold dead still, and pour its heart out in song.

It seems to be hung there on an invisible string, so still does it hold itself, and sometimes it seems that the string is being slowly wound up as the bird climbs in its hover. The song rolls on and on, and it is one of the great sounds of the spring. We hear it less often than we used to, because of changes in farming practice, but there are still plenty of sky-larks to lift our hearts in that extraordinary way.

Often you hear the first skylark of the year on a poor, dull day that has little to recommend it; but something moves within the skylark and he is up there and singing, while the observer on the ground wags his head in wonder and murmurs, "You must be out of your mind."

I once heard a piece of piano music based on the skylark's song; not a musical interpretation of the bird, like the wonderful pieces by Olivier Messiaen, but a strict musical rendering of a skylark in action. The skylark was, in fact, nothing less than the composer. Two more facts: it was an extraordinarily difficult piece to play, and neither musicians nor musicologists quite knew what to make of it. It was complex, at times harsh, at times sweet, very contemporary in sound, a strong and challenging piece of music.

It didn't sound much like a skylark, because the song had been slowed down. When a recording of a skylark is slowed down, its true complexity becomes clear. That is because birds are able to distinguish much shorter intervals of sound than humans. At the touch of a switch, the thrilling number of notes is revealed, and with it, the skylark's love of repetition and variation.

The skylark, having reached and sustained his peak, spirals down, still singing, until at the end he makes a silent parachute drop down to the place he is defending and advertising: his territory, to which he will lure a mate, feed and rear a brood of skylarks.

And when that job is done, it is as if the Technicolor bird reverts to monochrome, and he resumes his job as the drab, ground-based skulker. And you would think, if you saw him and did not know, that to him, the sky was an utterly alien environment.

15. Kestrel

Kestrels don't actually spend all that much time in the sky – not when compared to a swift, anyway. But the sky is where we mostly notice them: a stationary, cross-shape miraculously hanging in the air at the side of a motorway. That motorway habit makes them one of Britain's most easily seen birds, and the kestrel is the most frequently noticed bird of prey by a long way.

Bird of prey: there is something thrilling about just these three words. There is always something stirring about a bird of prey. It is a hard thing, to make a living by catching things. In order to do it, a bird must be exceptionally talented, for he has to confound creatures that have evolved precisely to escape from such hunters as himself.

We are right to thrill at birds of prey. A bird of prey is, by definition, rare. Food supplies make sure of that. There are not enough small creatures around to make kestrels as common as wrens and chaffinches. A bird of prey needs a relative abundance of prey in order to survive. If an ecosystem can support a bird of prey, it means that the ecosystem is in fair shape. The sight of a bird of prey does not spell evil and destruction: it is a sign of achievement, and of hope.

And the kestrel is the bird of prey we see most of. Its exceptional talent is for stationary flight. It is a master, nothing less; the only large bird to have truly mastered the hover. In still air, it can hang, as if attached to the sky by a thread, with frenziedly delicate flutterings of its sharply angled wings. In a stiff wind, it can hold its place by gliding at the exact speed of the wind. It is such a complete master that it can glide on the spot: the bird perfectly still but for frequent and subtle alterations of its aerofoil surfaces, while the wind rushes by and holds the bird above the earth.

For the kestrel, the sky is an observation post. You can see him scan the ground as he hovers, looking for the faint signs that tell him there is something good beneath him. The descent is not

Kestrel

Where to look: *motorway verges*
When to look: *all year*
What to look for: *hover*
What to listen for: *shouted ki-ki-ki*
in late summer when young
kestrels go in for mad chases

dramatic at all; a kestrel doesn't go for the head-long stoop of falcons like the peregrine. Rather, it descends in a series of steps – a parachute, followed by a hovering pause for a second look, sometimes even a third. The final drop is swift, silent and decisive.

Mostly it hunts the short-tailed field vole. These tubby little animals make tunnels beneath rank and tousled grasses. You are only likely to set eyes on one if the cat contributes a corpse to the household; a round and sleek little thing, with a slightly teddy-bearish look to it.

But the kestrel is pretty versatile. It will take mammals on the ground, and invertebrates; it can also take birds on the wing. This is not what the kestrel is famous for, nor what it is best at, but it is still pretty effective at grabbing small birds with ambushes, darts, dives and dashes.

Its direct flight is flappy and not at all dashing, as you would expect from a falcon – though when there is a decent bit of wind, kestrels can be highly aerobatic. They also love to soar, rising on the up-currents of air, wings spread out and rounded, to make a very different silhouette to the one we are used to.

Kestrels are wonderful fliers, and flight inspires us humans. Open spaces are what kestrels like best, and they are able to make a living just about any-where they can stretch their wings: farmland, heathland, moorland, parkland, forest fringes and sand-dunes, as well as roadside verges. But they need a high perch, for much of their hunting is done by sitting still and looking – far more economical than flying, which consumes vast amounts of energy. Once you have got used to that hunched, long-tailed silhouette, you will see far more kestrels than before; sometimes upright, sometimes, rather confusingly, more or less horizontal.

Catch them in good light, and they blaze with colour, a sumptuous brick-orange. Males and females are different, with males having a blue-grey head and tail. Both have distinct rusty backs contrasting well with black-brown wing-tips. They can be noisy birds, as well. You are most likely to hear them in late summer, when the young birds get above themselves and start chasing each other about, making high and excited noises, playing gang warfare games across the skies and shouting "kee-kee-kee".

Kestrels are clever and adaptable birds, and have got used to working in man-made environments, which explains why we see them so often. They don't live in the sky, but the sky is where you see them, and where they do what they do best.

Mallard

Where to look: *any bit of water. Once seen in trios over mantelpieces, now almost extinct in this environment*
When to look: *all year*
What to look for: *green head, orange feet*
What to listen for: *quack quack*

Fresh water

16. Mallard

Someone once told me that, so far as he was concerned, there were three kinds of birds: (a) little fluttery ones, (b) big flappy ones and (c) ducks. Most of us have a very clear idea of what the word duck means, and it is mallard.

The mallard is the duck for all seasons. As we take our first look at water birds, we must marvel at the mallard, because it is the duck for all waters. You can see mallards on the open sea, you can see them on the smallest ponds, you can see them on every sort of water in between.

Mallards are the ducks that you feed with scraps of bread, the ducks of the concrete-fringed park lake. But mallards can also be found leading a wilder, less circumscribed existence, bobbing in the waves of coastal waters, roosting miles out on a freezing reservoir in winter, foraging in the backwaters of a summer river, flying over a salt marsh with direction and purpose.

They are the ducks of everywhere and the ducks of everyman. Apart from Muscovy ducks, which originated in South America, mallards are the ancestors of all domestic ducks, from Indian runners to Aylesbury ducks; selectively bred for meat, eggs, docility, herdability, and looks. Often, domestic ducks escape and join the wild mallards, and you see complicated hybrids: dodgy mallards and scruffy Aylesburys. They regularly take the form of the vicar duck: a dark bird with an exaggerated white collar.

These variable half-and-halfers seem designed to confuse bad birdwatchers, particularly as they don't appear in a lot of field guides. But it's a fair rule that any untidy and disreputable looking duck is a wild-domestic mallard hybrid. Chuck him some bread and turn your attention to a real mallard.

Male and female are very different. The mallard drake is a bird of outrageous handsomeness, with his iridescent, bottle-green head, startlingly contrasted with his yellow beak, a chestnut breast, slim white collar, black and white stern with a dandified curly tail. The females are brown and speckly, but, like the males, they have a bluey-purpley patch on the wings: discreet in the female, part of the package of gaudiness in the male. Both have bright orange feet. Up in the air, the mallards wingbeats barely rise above body level. Females are dark brown but show white below each wing.

I should mention here that, in late summer, the males go into a moult and are briefly flightless. It stands to reason that at this time they want to be less noticeable. So they go into eclipse. That means that they look like females, but they keep their yellow beaks. It is easy to distinguish them from real females, then; and to mention that this bird is an eclipse male mallard can hardly fail to impress.

Males and female mallards look different and they also sound different. It is a wild idea to get used to, but it is only the females that make the authentic "quack-quack". The male is less noisy, and softer.

Mallards are everywhere. The reason for this is something we have met before; in fact, it is beginning to establish something of a pattern. Mallards are tolerant of humans and they are very adaptable. Those two things are the way to prosper on a planet so utterly dominated by humans: the shy specialists suffer while the brash jacks-of-all-trades prosper.

They are dabbling ducks, and they feed by upending in the water: bums up, beaks down beneath the surface. Up tails all, just as the poem in *The Wind in the Willows* says. But, for mallards, dabbling is just the start of it: they will feed from the surface; the young mallards will dive; and mallards of all ages will feed on land, too, for they are strong and confident walkers. They will graze like geese, and nip bits off potatoes if they can find them. In fact they eat a massive range of stuff: seeds, buds and leaves of water plants and land plants, insects, snails, worms, frogs, fish, even birds and mammals. They are not what you'd call fussy.

That tolerance and adaptability has made them very suitable for domestication, but it has also meant that they can make a living in a huge range of different places. They are highly prized as food items, by every decent-sized predator including humans, but they are smart and have well-developed escape ploys, including a steeply rising flight from water – almost a vertical take-off.

The males can be quarrelsome among themselves, especially in the spring, the big time of the year for breeding. They like loud, splashing chases, and at times they will fight quite seriously. They are noisy, confident birds, and if you have a patch of water, mallards will be the most effective birds in the place.

17. Tufted duck

Buoyant. That's a tufty. Well, tufted duck, to be formal, but the name always sounds more like tufty duck, and there is something inspiringly matey about a tufty: we are on nickname terms with the bird at first glance. I have given the tufties a full chapter to themselves, rather than tack them on to the end of the mallards as merely a different kind of duck. That's because tufties are so engaging and noticeable, and to add them as an afterthought would be a kind of insult, and I would not willingly insult a tufty.

Tufties are hugely likeable. There is something about them that commands the attention, something that brings an involuntary smile to the face when you set eyes on them. It is something to do with that buoyancy; the way they bobble on the surface of the water like a cork and seem merrily immune to the chills and buffets of life.

They are diving ducks. (Mallards are from a different group, called dabbling ducks.) And this gives the tufties a different outline in the water: tail tucked down low and out of sight, more compact. But all the same, there is nothing sleek and stylish about a tufty; they don't look like a masterpiece of hydrodynamic efficiency. They look like toys – the kind you hold under the bath water and then let spring back to the surface with a splash: rotund, cheerful and utterly indomitable.

The tufties are great divers, and they do most of their foraging underwater. They dive with a merry 'ere-we-go rolling forward action, and they come bursting back out again as if fired from the bottom by catapult – breaking the surface with a little splash just like a toy, the beadlets of water vanishing from their backs no sooner than they appear – rolling, in fact, like water off a duck's back. A duck keeps its feathers well covered with oil from its preen gland: they are proofed and reproofed. A tufty emerges from a dive as dry as when it started.

They can stay underwater for a remarkably long time for so buoyant a bird: not much short of half a

Tufted duck

Where to look: *deeper water than a mallard*
When to look: *all year*
What to look for: *bouyant black and white duck*
What to listen for: *not much*

minute. And they can get down to around 14 metres – hard indeed, for a tufty must work to stay under. These talents mean that the tufty can feed in different places to a mallard. For a mallard, the stuff more than a couple of feet below the surface is out of reach, but it's right where the tufty wants it.

That, by the way, is how all this business of species works: mallards have the shallows and the places where plants grow near the surface, but the next layer of stuff is there for the tufties – two different ways of making a living, two different species.

The tufty dives for plant and animal materials, seeds, insects, molluscs. It is far more a specialist than the mallard. It can't work in very deep water – nothing deeper than 15 metres – and it doesn't forage on land. But within its band, it is very efficient and effective. Tufties will come to park ponds, as well, preferring to stay a little deeper than the mallards, and they give delight because, for most people, they are the second kind of duck they can distinguish.

The drake tufties are wonderfully unmistakable: bold black and white, with a large black head that shows hints of green and purple in good light, a natty little tuft of feathers at the back of the head and a shining golden eye. The female is a rather uniform brown, with the same glittering eye, and just a bump where the male has his tuft.

There are many other ducks, of course, and I wish you joy as you explore them and their natures, and their different ways of living: the whistling of wigeon, the ponderousness of a shoveler, the elegance of pintail. But ducks start with mallards and tufties.

Canada goose

Where to look: *any decent expanse of water, parks*
When to look: *all year*
What to look for: *big bird, black neck, white chinstrap*
What to listen for: *obsessive honking in flight*

18. Canada goose

Always mistrust a person who dislikes Canada geese. It is an opinion that seems to me like a revelling in an all-too-rare opportunity for licensed xenophobia. It is considered deeply wrong to say that you dislike on sight people with non-English ancestry, that you hate people with blackish and brownish skins. But it is considered perfectly OK to express a hearty dislike of such former foreigners as the Canada goose.

Canada geese look foreign, and they have a foreign name. They stand out from the crowds and are noisy and obstructive: things that are helpful if you want to make yourself a target for casual dislike. But they have been with us for around 300 years. They bred at Versailles during the time of Louis XIV. An 18th-century writer wrote of Canada geese: "In England, likewise, they are thought a great ornament of the pieces of water in many gentlemen's seats, where they are very familiar and breed freely."

Canada geese are part of our lives, and we might as well make the most of them. Why not? They are among the most magnificent birds in Britain. This magnificence is something they best express in flight: strong, direct, low, and all the time calling to each other in raucous bugling voices: "Ah-hunghh! Ah-hunghh!"

They mostly fly in groups, favouring the classic V-formation, in which each bird has his passage through the air rendered that little bit easier by the bird in front. It's about air resistance; cyclists on the Tour de France operate according to the same policy. Canada geese will also fly in diagonals or even straight lines, but the V-formation is best, and is always accompanied by a great din – something that sounds like mutual encouragement to keep the formation tight and effective. And they take turns as leader, for one goose can't do all the hard work.

British Canada geese have a great feeling for human populations, and rapidly figure out how to work in proximity to human dwellings and in harmony with human demands. It is as if their natural habitat were ornamental lakes, a world away from the tough, migratory life led by Canada geese in North America.

They are unmistakable: big burly birds with long black necks and an unmissable white chinstrap. They live on plants and will feed on land, as well as on the water. They frequently graze on playing-fields, which does not make them popular – the saying "as loose as a goose" is not there just for the rhyme. Geese in general take in a lot of plant material and pass it through the system fairly quickly. It is logical, then, that rugby players tend not to be Canada goose fans.

These geese are confident walkers, moving with a rolling gait rather like a boxer moving to the scales for the weigh-in. On the water they feed by ducking their heads with bendy necks, almost as sinuous as swans. They produce long flotillas of Canada goslings, and at this time it is impossible not to find the species a charming addition to British life.

There is one other readily seen goose in this country, and that's the greylag goose: big and pale grey-brown, with orange beak and pink legs. It is the ancestor of the white farmyard goose, and any white goose you bump into is a domestic goose that has gone feral. The Chinese probably bred their own domestic goose – called, not unnaturally, the Chinese goose – from something called the swan goose; these Chinese geese also occasionally crop up among wild birds.

There are other geese to see in this country, and all geese, it seems to me, are birds that have a special talent for lifting the heart. They are water birds who are seen at their best in the air; a skein of geese, flying with such power and purpose, cannot help but give the observer a sudden rush of hope. A goosey flypast seems to fill the air with aspiration and confidence, and that is truly inspiring.

It is the Canada geese that attract the attention, because they are so noticeable and so good at human haunts. They are the geese you are most likely to see from a window, train, car, office, in the course of a working day, moving from one feeding ground to another, bugling importantly to each other, and keeping the formation tight. Ah-hunghh! Ah-hunghh!

19. Swan

Swans are essentially massive. They look imposing on the water. They look positively gigantic when they step on to land with their awkward don't-mess-with-me waddle. They are conscious of their size, too – well aware of their ability to scare just about everything they have a mind to. They have a reputation for aggression which, even if you have made the standard allowance for exaggeration, is still pretty impressive.

They are also birds of grace and splendour, and they turn up on every decent-sized bit of water, no matter how many people are about. There are three species of swan you are likely to see in Britain, but, for our purposes, it's the mute swan that matters.

They don't need describing: huge and white and long-necked. Sometimes they hold their necks straight and beak angled down, sometimes their necks are curled in a pronounced and elegant S-shape – a swan-neck, in fact.

Their history has been tied up with humans for nine centuries. For a long time, they were semi-domesticated birds, whose needs were catered for because they were considered good for eating. Plenty of meat on a swan, certainly.

Swans have become accustomed to human life, even if they must do their own foraging these days. They take food from beneath the surface where, obviously enough, they can reach far deeper than any other surface feeder – dipping down with the long snaky neck, or even upending totally, like a daft and gigantic duck. They take vegetation, and what they like best is large, open lakes with lots of shallow places for feeding in. They will also graze on land, and will strut about in a rather self-important fashion on their huge black feet.

They are strong fliers, but it takes a fair bit of work to get themselves up into the air. They are pretty close to the top limit of weight for a flying bird, and are comfortably the heaviest flying birds seen in this country. Their take-off requires a decent runway, like an overloaded troop-carrying aircraft.

Mute swan

Where to look: *any decent expanse of water*
When to look: *all year*
What to look for: *enormous white bird*
What to listen for: *throbbing of wings in flight*

For this, they choose an empty stretch of lake (if it's not empty, it soon will be once a swan starts making its charge) and run along it, eventually splashing on the surface, flapping like mad, until they have enough forward speed to make true flight possible. This high, stalling speed makes their landings fairly dramatic, too. They land on water, always, or they would crash and break their necks, and instead of stalling into the water, they make a kind of panicky water-skiing transition from air to water. It's dramatic stuff. Flight is a big deal for a swan, and it's not something they enter into lightly. But in flight they are strong and shockingly big, their long necks stretched out ramrod straight, the wings making a strange throbbing sound that you can hear up to two kilometres away.

In the breeding season, swans are notably aggressive to other birds. They are toughest on other adult swans: the younger, non-breeding birds retain their dirty, ugly-ducking look for good reason — as an advertisement of the fact that they are posing no threat to a breeding swan.

A swan in full threat display is one of the most awesome sights in world birdwatching. It raises up its wings like the sails of a galleon, pulls its head as far back into this fearsome mass of feathers as it can, fluffs up its neck, and gives out a stare like a blowtorch. It will then approach the object of its dislike. But it doesn't use the smooth, rhythmic paddle that it employs for normal occasions, first one webbed foot then the other. When it wants to look mean, it hooshes towards you in a series of menacing jerks, two feet together. All put together, this behaviour is called busking.

Swans will menace other swans, other water birds, and human beings, and if you don't get frightened off by the performance, they are perfectly capable of following up with physical assault. They have a fully justified confidence in their strength and their immensity.

A pair of swans will stick together for season after season, often for life – they go in for long-term relationships. But outside the breeding season, they forget about being the fastest beak on the lake, and become sociable, gathering in large groups when they can, sometimes of a hundred and more.

For all their warlike nature, they have become a byword for grace and peace; and they represent that mood just as well. Out in the middle of a lake, a swan doesn't have to look for a safe place. A swan is a safe place.

The other two species of swans come to this country in the winter after spending the summer in the far north, where they profit from the brief but teeming arctic summers. These are the whooper swan and the Bewick's swan; we will discuss the Bewick's at length later on (p245). The whooper and the Bewick's make up for the mute swans' general habit of silence – occasional snarls and hisses are about the only sound you get from them – with a complex vocabulary full of amazing honking and bugling.

But the swan that we know and understand best is the mute swan: majestic, self-certain, graceful, bellicose. A bird that stands for calm and beauty, just so long as you don't try and get in his way in April.

Woodland

20. Woodpecker

There are birds that the beginning birdwatcher thinks beyond his scope: too rare, too obscure, too difficult; something for the specialist, for the buff, for the true expert. As a boy, I always thought that the great-spotted woodpecker came into that category, something so fabulously rare that it was more or less mythical.

Years later, I discovered that great-spotted woodpeckers are all around us. Just about wherever there are mature deciduous trees, you will find great spotted woodpeckers. They are pretty common; just a little on the shy side. Seeing them requires a bit of a knack: one of the great ambitions of this book is to help the beginner birdwatcher acquire it.

Green woodpecker

Where to look: *on the ground,*
on grassy country near trees
When to look: *all year*
What to look for: *yellow bum*
in flight
What to listen for: *hysterical*
laughter

The easiest way, of course, is to feed the birds in the garden. Great-spots are occasional visitors to the bird-feeder; certainly the most exotic birds that turn up for the daily freebie. And they look outrageous: big, flamboyantly black and white, with a wild touch of red on the back end of the underbody. Males also have a touch of red on the back of their heads. They are sumptuous and dramatic birds; a real treat for those with gardens close to big trees.

And you wonder: how is it that such a gaudy bird could be overlooked? Surely they would stand out on a tree trunk like splash of white paint. But they don't. That flashy colour scheme is actually a clever form of camouflage. There are two kinds of camouflage: the kind that blends in with the surrounding – cryptic camouflage – and the kind that seeks to break up the outline. That's disruptive camouflage, and if you try and look up at a tree that contains a great-spotted woodpecker, you'll see how effective it is.

How did you know it was there in the first place? This is the great knack. All it takes is to open your ears to one sound: "Pik! Pik!" That is the contact call of the great-spotted woodpecker, the call they make to each other, the one that means, "I'm here, where are you?" It is a very distinct sound and once you have got the hang of it, you suddenly realise that the world is full of great-spotted woodpeckers. You can learn it by listening around big trees, or more easily, from a recording (there are details of how to find recordings in the back of the book). Buy one, listen to the pik, and then walk out of your house and find a few trees. Soon you will hear it and recognise it; soon your life will be full of woodpeckers. That is a very considerable miracle for a minutely small outlay of money and time.

And then you can see them, once you know they are there – generally in flight, moving from one stand of trees to another, frequently calling "pik!" as they go. It is a very distinctive flight: a few wing beats, and then the wings are closed, the birds dips down, only to flap and rise again, in a series of steep switchbacks. Again, once you have got the hang of it, it is unmistakable, and as they fly over, you might get a glimpse of the red underside, and then see them swooping upwards to slap themselves into the trunk or the branch they were aiming for.

In the spring you will hear them drum – short and powerful. There are three regularly seen wood-peckers in this country: the green woodpecker which scarcely ever drums and, when it does so, the drum is feeble; the lesser-spotted woodpecker, which is *really* hard to see – this one drums longer and higher and softer; and the great-spots which you will see in woodlands, but also in parklands, copses, gardens, anywhere you find decent trees.

The green woodpeckers also need decent trees, but they are, a little surprisingly, most often seen on the ground. This is because they feed on ants; they use their beaks to dig into ants' nests and a long tongue – nearly four inches – to slurp into the holes they have dug and to drink up the ants.

You are most likely to see these birds flying away when you have disturbed them; and you are mostly aware of a striking yellow bum, which is emphasised by an undulating flight that is notably similar to the great-spot. They are splendidly and unapologetically green (cryptic camouflage), with vivid red heads.

And they laugh. A ringing, accelerating laugh, something that echoes around the trees in the spring. It's called a yaffle, or yaffling – a laugh that adds a hilarious joy to the rising of the spring.

One of the problems of birdwatching in woodland is that it can be hard to watch any birds. The trees keep getting in the way. They haven't yet invented a pair of binoculars that can see through branches and leaves and, up in the canopy, birds are out of sight. But they make up for that with their voices, and if you tune into the "pik!" and to the yaffle, you will have woodpeckers wherever you go, for as long as you are near the right trees.

21. Jay

A jay is perhaps the most amazing bird in Britain. That is because it amazes more people than any other species. It is another common but shy bird, and it regularly takes non-birdwatchers by surprise. It is an outrageous looking thing – those unfamiliar with the idea of a jay can't help but conclude that they have been privileged to see one of the world's rarest and most exotic birds. A writer called WH Hudson once called the jay "the British bird of paradise". Non-birdwatchers frequently tell bird-watchers that they have seen a "funny bird" in their gardens: Bill Oddie claims that 99 per cent of all layman's funny birds are jays.

A jay is utterly bewildering. It can look bright

Jay

Where to look: *oak trees*
When to look: *all year*
What to look for: *outrageously gaudy bird*
What to listen for: *furious screaming, cloth-ripping screech*

pink, alternatively, it can flash bright blue, and it can also look elaborately black and white. It is the more startling because it normally keeps itself to itself in woody places. When it turns up in a garden it looks absurdly gaudy and thrillingly exotic.

The jay is a member of the crow family, as the hefty size and dagger bill might have told you. But never mind your traditional crowish black – jays are a buffy pink, with vivid blue patches on the wings. They also have a pale, streaky crown that can look, in certain lights, like a significant crest. And when you see one flying away, as you often do, they have a highly noticeable white bum, and white wing-patches as well.

They don't often show themselves in all their glory, however. They just like to do so every now and then, to startle non-birdwatchers. But if you have anything to do with oak trees in your life, you are likely to have something to do with jays. Jays and oak trees have a deep and important bond.

Walk through an oak wood, and you hear the most terrible hoarse screaming. It seems to shake the trees, a violent and extraordinary din. That's a jay. It's not even essential to learn that one from a recording – anything that screams in a really intemperate fury is a jay.

Like the other crows, jays feed on all kinds of

stuff: insects – especially beetles – bigger game if they can get hold of it, larvae, seeds. But they have a special thing for acorns. They can make a living in other sorts of woodland, but the jay's heartland is an oak wood. It is as near a specialist as that wild band of freebooters, the crows, have come up with.

The jay is a great burier of acorns. It is actually pretty good at remembering where it has put them as well. Think about it: it would hardly be good survival strategy, to expend energy on burying hundreds of acorns if you were unable to find them again. The buried acorns represent a defence against hard times to come; the jay is a very effective bird at exploiting his chosen environment.

On the other hand, you might prefer to say that the jay's chosen environment is very good at exploiting the jay. Because, even with the best memory in the world, a jay is not going to unbury every single acorn. Some of them will get overlooked, and they will germinate in the following spring, and make their determined bid to become a mature oak tree. A long-term ambition, of course. But when these acorns are planted in places away from the main body of the oak wood, then the wood has a chance to spread.

So you can say that the jay is ripping off the oaks by stealing their seeds; but the oaks are stealing the jay's services, bribing him with acorns so that he helps the wood to spread. Not, of course, that either of them thinks things through in those terms; but that is how it all works, all the same. Jays and oaks exploit each other in a very effective way.

Jays, for all their shyness, have a bold and jaunty air when they come into sight. That is helped by the dashing black moustache worn by both sexes, and the gleaming, almost dazzling eye. On the ground, they are exceptionally strong hoppers, bounding about with pogo-stick enthusiasm, allied to a great sense of preoccupation and purpose.

They also do a great service to humankind. Because of their extraordinary looks, and their wacky colours, they attract the eye of the non-bird-watcher, and persuade him to look that little bit more closely at birds. Jays have probably done more than any other bird to turn non-birdwatchers into birdwatchers. We owe them thanks for that; almost enough to forgive them the ear-splitting din they make from some secluded place high up in an oak tree. Ah, but no – it is fine noise, a fine wild noise. The jay is a beautifully and uninhibitedly colourful bird, so it is only fair that it should make an uninhibitedly raucous and ugly din. It would hardly be fair if it were to sing like a nightingale.

22. Sparrowhawk

Sorry, but you're on your own here. Sparrowhawk
is the bird that no one can show you. There! What?
Sparrowhawk! Where is it? Gone. If you see a bird
appear and disappear in an instant: well, it might
have been a sparrowhawk.

Sparrowhawks have their being in suddenness.
They make their living by means of ambush and
chase. Their food is almost entirely other birds. A
very tough option to take because, as you will have
noticed, birds can fly, and they are very good indeed
at doing so.

Once a bird knows that you are after him, you've
got no chance. The only way you are going to bring
it off is by grabbing the bird before it's ready for you.

Sparrowhawk

Where to look: *woodland, gardens*
When to look: *all year*
What to look for: *a flash of lightning*
What to listen for: *cat-like mewing
from hungry, young birds waiting for
food-bringing parents*

And so sparrowhawks have a hunting pattern that is based on speed and stealth. They use cover: trees, hedges, walls, slopes and hollows.

They are essentially woodland birds, but they operate at their best around woodland edge, glades, clearings. They will exploit hedges in a brilliant fashion: swapping from one side of the hedge to the other in brisk forays designed to flush out, frighten and capture smaller birds.

They can get through impossibly small gaps. I have heard tales of a sparrowhawk flying through the gap between two suburban houses, a passage a scant foot wide, bursting into the garden on the far side in the hope of startling birds on the far side.

Sparrowhawks are not particularly comfortable around humans and human haunts, but their speed and agility means that they can make sudden dashing raids on gardens, and then clear off again to places where they are happier. I have received many a heart-rending letter from nice people who put out food for the birds, and then feel guilty when a sparrowhawk bursts in and takes a blue tit just as he is tucking into the peanuts.

I sympathise with the distress; but blue tits eat caterpillars, which is not all that pleasant for the caterpillar. It's not nice, no, but then, as I have said before, the fact is that nature is not nice – beautiful, thrilling, challenging, enthralling and altogether wonderful, yes – but nice, no. Sparrowhawks eat nice birds, just as lions eat nice antelopes.

Both sights can be distressing. I know, I have seen both, in extraordinary detail. It is all the sadder when a sparrowhawk fails to kill the bird with his first attack, as is quite often the case. His victim then must die a piteous and protracted death during the plucking and the eating. Still, that is the way that life works; and anyway, the blue tit, whatever else you can say, has certainly had a better life than a battery chicken. Humans are much crueller than sparrowhawks.

I won't give you a detailed description of the sparrowhawk's plumage because you are extremely unlikely to see it. Sparrowhawks are mostly seen in explosions of action: a dark, menacing shape, a blur of speed. The male is a very natty little bird if you ever see him still, bricky-orange underneath. The female is a fair bit larger, and lacks the colour.

This difference in size means a difference in diet: the males eat mainly tits and finches, the females go for thrushes and starlings. Both will have hunting perches, and will work a hunting route from favourite perch to favourite perch; from these they will launch their raids and ambushes. They are so agile they will catch a rising bird by inverting in the air and taking it from below with upraised talons. And they will sit in the middle of a hedge, rather unfairly waiting for small birds to come past.

Their flight from place to place is pretty distinctive: a very pronounced flap-flap-glide. They are essentially a different shape from a kestrel, the other commonly seen small bird of prey in this country, but they can look irritatingly similar when they pinch in the tips of their wings.

Occasionally, you will see a sparrowhawk soaring. This will often be very high. In a soar, the wings look short, stubby and round, and very un-kestrel-like. You will quite often see a lone sparrowhawk being mobbed by a crow or two as they soar, an intriguing sight, for the sparrowhawk seems not to mind the attention too much. Instead, it dodges the assaults with the nonchalance of George Best evading a full-back.

They nest in woody areas, in well-grown trees, without too much disturbance. But they will turn up in all sorts of areas where there is food to be had, making forays from woodland to any place within easy commuting distance to pick up a meal.

Sparrowhawks don't make much noise, not when they are grown up. But in the high summer, you might just hear what sounds like a cat stuck up a tree. You might even hear what sounds like three or four cats stuck up neighbouring trees. This is a family of young sparrowhawks, old enough to leave the nest but not old enough to find food on their own. They are there making hunger-calls, waiting for their parents to come back with a feathery meal.

Sparrowhawks are by no means rare, but always hard to see. They are sudden birds, and they will put a beginning birdwatcher on his mettle: a dark shape so close to the ground it's a wonder it doesn't strike its wings on the down beat; another dark shape that materialises in front of you as you walk along a hedge, and then vanishes just as suddenly. Sparrowhawks give the thrill of the unexpected to an ordinary walk. That is their point. If they weren't unexpected, they wouldn't be able to survive.

23. Owl

Here is one bird sound you don't need to learn. The wobbling, wavering hoot – we've heard it in a million horror films, and heard it in real life often enough: whoooooooooo! Everybody knows that's the noise an owl makes. To be specific, it's the noise a tawny owl makes. When you have mature trees and darkness, then you are likely to hear tawny owls at some time. You are not so very likely to see them, but never mind, it's nice to know they are there. Tawnies are hard to see because they are seriously nocturnal.

Some owls – barn owls in particular – like dawn and dusk; others, confusingly, are happy in pure daylight, the short-eared owl being the best example. The tawny is a true night-owl: it really doesn't do very much at all during the daylight hours.

But here's a surprise. Tawny owls don't go: "too-whit too-whoo". Rather, they "too-whit" *and* they go "too-whoo". Broadly speaking, the wobbly hoot is the sound used to announce the possession of territory – a warning for other tawnies to keep away. The "too-whit" is a contact call: "I'm here, where are you?"

It is more often written down as "ke-wick", and it is a very good sound to learn, as it is not the sort of sound you expect from an owl. In fact, for years, I thought it was the call of a rabbit, thanks to some spectacularly poor information I was given. It's a nice sound to imitate. If you get it right, you some-times get owls answering back, which is for some reason deeply gratifying, if perplexing to the poor owls.

It's a sound you hear quite often if you live near stands of mature trees – which makes sense, when you think about it. Owls operate in the dark, so they can't easily see where their partners have got to. And in the autumn, when young owls leave the nest and seek a territory of their own, they make the "ke-wick" call a lot – and often provoke a frenzied response from the owners of the territory.

Tawny Owl

Where to look: *woodland*
When to look: *dead of night, all year*
What to look for: *a shadow in the trees*
What to listen for: *Hammer Horror film soundtrack*

Owls are very protective of their own piece of woodland, their own territories. This is not just for the love of possession. An owl's best asset in making a living is knowledge – in-depth detailed knowledge – of its own place. You can find your own way around your own house in the dark because you know the place well. An owl has the same relationship with his own patch.

And it puts this knowledge to use by knowing the best hunting perches, and how to get from one to the other in the dark. It knows that if it drops onto something below, it will not damage itself on unexpected obstacles. If you frighten a tawny owl, it might well panic and fly into a tree. It's not the owl's vision that is exceptional, it is the map it keeps in its head.

Hearing is the tawny's best hunting tool, not sight. It can hear what goes on beneath him, and use that knowledge to drop silently and precisely onto the sound.

Tawnies take rodents, and shrews, and even young rabbits. They also take bats. They will take birds from roost or from the nest, and they won't turn their beaks up at worms and beetles. They have even been seen catching fish.

Should you catch a glimpse of a tawny, you are rewarded with a fine sight: a big brown bird with a big head, and a noticeably round face – facial disc, to use the proper term. They always have a sleepy, rotund air to them. The silhouette is very distinctive; the expression indeed seems curiously wise, and rather gentle.

Trees are essential to the tawny owl, trees with hollows for nesting in. They don't come into contact with humans much, because they are so much creatures of the dark, but they are happy in parks, gardens and graveyards. They are used in horror films, not because they are in themselves horrifying, but because the hoot is a sound you associate so much with darkness. "Too-whoo": it is almost the sound of blackness.

Tawnies will hunt on the wing, if their territory involves some open country. But they are most completely themselves in the routines of woodland life – moving from one perch to the next, pausing, listening, and dropping in glides or silent flaps. All owls are capable of completely silent flight, with feathery mufflers stifling any give-away swish. They are secret, silent and surreptitious.

But love of the dark does make them noisy when they are not at the sharp end of a hunt. Use your ears and you will find your owls. The "too-whoo" you know; learn the "too-whit" and there will be many more owls in your life. And if you did hear a tawny owl going "too-whit too-whoo", it was almost certainly two birds – a male answering a female "too-whit" with a nice wavering "too-whoo".

Barn owl
Where to look: *open country, field edges*
When to look: *dusk, all year*
What to look for: *a big white bird flying low and slow*
What to listen for: *strangulated scream*

Countryside

24. Crow

Crows are clever. There are some that consider crows the most highly evolved birds, and if you define high evolution as similarity to human beings – a somewhat dubious notion – then crows are the tops. They have an adaptability and a smartness that humans relate to very strongly.

Humans also respond to crows with dislike. They frequently find them sinister, swaggering, insensitive, cruel, and far too prone to treating the place as if they owned it; traits every bit as human-like as intelligence.

Crows are black birds that you see all around the countryside. There are three species of them – four in the far west and north.

Carrion crow

Where to look: *open country, often in flight*
When to look: *all year*
What to look for: *unrelieved black*
What to listen for: *an angry triple-caw*

Well, to be accurate, the crow tribe also includes jays and magpies, along with the much rarer chough, with its bright red beak. But it is the black birds that we commonly refer to as crows. Everyone knows a crow: a black bird, flying past on its characteristic beeline, rowing across the sky with strong rhythmic beats. There always seems a sense of purpose when a crow is going from A to B.

The number one crow is the carrion crow – birdwatchers frequently refer to them just as "crows". This is a seriously black bird: black feathers, black feet, black beak. Its caw is loud and harsh and rather angry, and is frequently heard in threes.

Like the other black crows, the carrion crow is most often seen over open countryside and, generally, two at a time, since they are keen on being half of a pair. They go in for wide-ranging foraging, and will eat just about anything, from seeds to dead animals. They are talented at exploiting opportunities. Grain, small animals and birds, eggs, carrion, scraps – the crows are committed generalists, determined dodgers of the tender trap of specialisation.

They often feed on open ground and have a great variety of different ways of doing it: surface picking, turning over stones and dung, surface probing, pouncing, digging and deep probing. They will open milk bottles to steal a drink. They will hang upside down from peanut bags, unembarrassed by the ungainly, flapping spectacle they make of themselves. They have been seen pulling up fishing lines and hammering at dead branches like a woodpecker. They will hang from sunflower heads to get at the seeds; they will perch on the back of animals and search for ticks, like birds of the African bush. The account of the different kinds of food they eat takes up a column and a half in the renowned nine-volume reference work, *The Birds of the Western Palaearctic*.

They are, then, birds to admire. Rooks are less resourceful, but still highly successful. Rooks are more often found in flocks than carrion crows — there are various versions of the saying that one rook is crows, but two crows is rooks. The idea is sound, but it's not reliable: crows are not averse to a bit of flocking, and rooks are perfectly capable of coping as singletons. All the same, a crowd of big black birds is more likely to be rooks.

But the face is the give-away — the face and the head. The rook's face and beak are pale parchment-grey, giving the bird a haggard, careworn, appearance — some go so far as to say a rather elderly look, like a scruffy, ageing undertaker in a shabby black suit. The shape of the head is different, too — seemingly all beak. Rooks have a little peaked forehead, while the crow has a longer, broader top to its head. Rooks have looser-looking body feathers, which give that black suit rather noticeably baggy trousers.

Rooks like agricultural land to forage on, with tall trees nearby to roost and nest in. And they like to do both in decent numbers when they can. Rooks love company. They caw to each other a great deal; a much more mellow, less irritable sound than that of the carrion crow. The sleepy cawing of a busy rookery in times of repletion is one of the great soothing sounds of the late spring – you'd hardly say that of a bunch of crows. Rooks also converse in a medley of squeaks and quiet trumpeting notes.

Rooks also like to feed perilously close to the edge of roads, perhaps looking for insects killed by cars. They will forage for scraps in unexpected places, including the carparks at motorway service stations.

The third black crow is the jackdaw – much smaller, jauntier, cheerier, cockier. This bird has a grey head with a black cap perched on the top, and a rather pigeon look to it in flight. Jackdaws can often be seen in mixed crow flocks. You can see the difference pretty clearly in flight: the jackdaw is much smaller, and takes two wing beats for every one of the larger crows. Slow crow, flap jack, as one mnemonic has it.

A jackdaw doesn't really need much looking for because it is a terribly gabby bird, and what it mostly says is "jack!" It is a clear and decisive utterance, often mixed up with unexpected high-pitched yelps. But any black birds that says "jack" is a jackdaw.

They too are clever and adaptable feeders. They like trees, but they can also make a living around cliffs and big buildings. They are wonderfully bold fliers, loving to ride the big winds, and they seem to do it for the simple pleasure of it. They will make huge vertical circles with scarcely a flap of the wings, for no apparent purpose save their relish of the wind, and their mastery of it.

I had better add a brief note about the hooded crow, and I'll try not to be confusing. In Ireland, the Isle of Man and northern Scotland, the usual crow is not black all over, but very contrasty, with a black head and black wings on a grey background. Therefore, they are called hooded crows, hoodies for short. At one time they were considered a different species, then they were thought to be the same species, because in the buffer zones between carrion crow and hooded crow territory, you get plenty of half-and-halfers, hybrids. But recently, scientists have begun to treat them as a separate species again. In other words, carrion and hooded crows are the same, except for the fact that they are different. Confusing, I know. Relish the difference and the wonder and complexity of it. And, more importantly, relish the flamboyant cleverness of the dourly dressed crow tribe.

Rook
Where to look: *trees, open fields, clumps of nests in big trees*
When to look: *all year*
What to look for: *crow with pale beak*
What to listen for: *mellow caw, often from roosting flocks*

25. Pheasant

Pheasants prosper in an alien land because people love to kill them. Never can a creature have survived so well because of its ability to die. This is a bizarre paradox, and it says many strange things about the way humans relate to their landscape and to the creatures that live in it.

Pheasants are everywhere in the organised and cultivated countryside. So they should be. Humans put them there – and they carry on putting them there. They have been here for centuries, since long before the invention of the shotgun. Pheasants are Asian by origin, but according to legend they were brought to Europe in 1300 BC by Jason and the Argonauts.

Pheasant

Where to look: *country roads; round birds on roadsides, flat birds on road surface*
When to look: *all year*
What to look for: *long tail; suicidal tendencies*
What to listen for: *in spring, a loud crowing followed by a wing-whir*

There is doubt and dispute about when exactly they came to this country, but documents indicate that pheasants got here before the Normans. They were semi-domestic birds at first, kept for food and for the pleasures of the hunt. From the 12th century onwards, they turn up with increasing frequency in poetry – generally in connection with hunting or eating. It seems that they established themselves as self-propagating feral birds round about the 15th century.

It is the spectacular looks, especially of the cock bird, that make them irresistible: the speckles, the coppery and bronzy tones of the body, the green head and red face, and the daring, swashbuckling Robin Hood tail. The female is quieter, with a shorter, more spiky tail and a plain brown head.

Pheasants are ground birds by inclination. They run well, and forage on the ground for seeds and insects. They are not fussy feeders and they will take a wide range of food. That makes them relatively easy to keep, and means that the wild or semi-wild birds don't find it difficult to survive. They have recently been pinpointed as a danger to British reptiles, for they eat prodigious quantities of slow worms and lizards.

They might have evolved in order to please a man with a shotgun. They get up to fly with great reluctance and, when they do, they keep low, because they have heavy bodies and do not have huge stamina. Thus a flushed pheasant becomes an instant target for what some people refer to as "sport".

Personally, I can't see the pleasure in blasting fat, half-tame birds to bits, especially when they are incompetent fliers. But it is better to be large-minded in these matters – and I'll tell you why.

Pheasants will forage anywhere they can find food; but, as Asian birds, they hate the wind and the wet. To be caught in the open in bad weather is a killer. In wintry conditions, they much prefer to skulk in wooded and sheltered places. And round many parts of the country, you find that the monotony of the agricultural landscape is broken up with small copses and little woods. These are places that have been left, mainly for the convenience of pheasants, so that the landowner can have the pleasure of shooting them. These days, he is more likely to rent out that pleasure – a modern farmer must make money where he can, and pheasant shooting is worth serious money.

These little chunks of woodland play a huge role in giving life to the agricultural countryside. A copse may shelter pheasants, but it will also hold blue tits and robins and wrens, and maybe the odd sparrowhawk as well. Without the blood lust for the lovely, ungainly pheasant, we would have a greatly impoverished countryside.

The male pheasant is very variable. You often see very dark and very pale birds. Some have a white collar, occasionally a very large one, many have no collar at all. They are very vocal birds. In spring, you hear the males making a loud crow, followed by a furious whirring of the wings – an almost comically self-important announcement of their magnificence, and their intention to hold onto this particular bit of territory.

They are also the most startling birds in the country – because of their habit of lying doggo until the very last minute, and then rising more or less vertically, right under your feet, with a ludicrous panicky tick-up, tick-up, tick-up, and a frenzied whirling of wings that look almost too small to take them up into the air.

You often see pheasants dead on the road. They seem hopelessly incapable of judging the speed of oncoming cars, or of assessing their dangerous potential – birds of astonishing naiveté. No doubt this is because so many pheasants are reared artificially and then released, and so many birds are shot. In shooting areas, pheasants don't live to a grand old age, so they have no chance of building up the wisdom that comes from experience. Instead, the population is constantly replenished by artificially reared birds.

It is a curiously synthetic way to run the countryside, particularly as gamekeeping practices involve the killing (sorry, that should be "control") of ground predators. Killing birds of prey is now, at least, illegal. It is a deeply peculiar business, all in all, but the pheasants are agreeable to look at, and the woods and copses that shelter them are rich and important. Pheasants are perpetually doomed birds, and they have given the countryside life.

Magpie

Where to look: *countryside, suburbs*
When to look: *all year*
What to look for: *two birds like a pair of co-respondent shoes*
What to listen for: *jungling chacka-chacka-chacka*

26. Magpie

Let's be logical about this. I have lived in the English countryside for nearly 20 years. In that time, the countryside population of songbirds has decreased sharply. The only conclusion you can draw from this is that I am personally responsible for the decline in the population of songbirds.

You could, at a stretch, argue that it is nothing but a coincidence, that the songbird would have declined whether I lived in the country or not. But hell, there I am, and there the songbirds aren't. So the only thing to do is to go right ahead and blame me.

Actually, people don't blame me for the decline in songbirds. They blame the magpie, and they blame the magpie with just as much logic. It has become one of the accepted truths about the countryside: magpies have eaten all the songbirds. That is because magpies are evil – and Something Should Be Done About It.

The RSPB gets more correspondence on the subject than any other matter, and its breaks the hearts of good hard-working conservationists. The remorseless repetition of the question has them on their knees, begging: "Please, please just think about the issue, if only for a second or two." So let us take a brief trawl through something very rarely used in the anti-magpie argument. facts.

Magpie numbers have doubled since 1970, though the population has been stable since 1990. Since 1970, countryside populations of songbirds have dropped. And yes, magpies do eat the eggs and nestlings, and, to human eyes, this is a brutal and distressing idea. However, it is no more brutal than the fact that, when a male lion takes over a new pride, the first thing he does is kill all the cubs. Nature does not exist in order to seek the moral approval of humankind; it is about surviving, breeding, and the ultimate goal of becoming an ancestor.

Point to consider: songbirds have declined at the same rate in magpie-heavy areas as they have in magpie-light areas. This is a crystal-clear indication that something other than magpies is at the bottom of the decline. In fact, some species of songbirds — songbirds that are very much on the magpie menu — have actually increased: chaffinch, blackcap. Other songbirds have declined, even though they are not on the magpie menu. Hole-nesters are magpie-proof, but despite the apparent advantage, the tree sparrow and the starling are both in decline. And you can't blame the magpie for that.

Let's say that there are 30 species of birds whose nests are vulnerable to magpies. Their population adds up to 45.3 million pairs, and between them, they produce 472.4 million fledglings and eggs every year. Are we suggesting that the songbird decline has happened because magpies take more than 427.1 million eggs and fledglings a year?

No: the magpie is the most colossal red herring. Songbirds have declined for a complex mixture of reasons, most of them to do with changes in farming practice. There is less food around, and less suitable habitat, and that is the heart of the matter. A wholesale cull of magpies would be neither practical, nor sustainable, nor effective. What we must do to reverse the decline in songbirds is to support all moves for more environmentally sensitive farming. But that is complex and unsatisfying, so the evil magpie gets the blame. The fuss about magpies has done absolutely nothing but divert attention from the real problems that affect farmland birds.

I haven't got round to describing a magpie for you, but then you know what they look like already: black and white birds of piratical mien, whose loud and regularly heard voice is a harsh, mocking cackle. They play the part of the villain very well; and that is more than half of the problem. Magpies are in truth canny and resourceful birds, as you would expect from a member of the crow family, and their favoured food is insects and other invertebrates, fruit and seeds. One for sorrow, two for joy, people say – a superstition that is weighted very much in favour of those who hold it, because magpies spend most of their lives as half of a pair, and the two spend most of their time together.

They fly like paper aeroplanes, and are stunning to look at in very good light. Their feathers are iridescent with metallic greens, blues and purples. They make their living in a thoroughly respectable way, even if some aspects of this offend human ideas of what is fitting. And the most important point of all: they are not in any way to blame for the fact that we humans have made a series of bad choices in the way we manage our countryside.

27. Lapwing

I'll try not to gush. But you see, lapwings are real favourites of mine. Their glorious individualistic charm has increased vastly as their population has declined. You are so very glad to see them when you see them.

Lapwings are waders, which means that they stand on comparatively long legs. They look strongly black and white at any sort of distance. Any time outside the spring, you will see them in flocks – they like to be in seriously huge numbers but, with their decline, they can turn up in handfuls as well as hundreds.

They are countryside birds, with a liking for damp, badly drained fields. Changes in farming practice are the main causes of their decline. But you can also find them around the coast, on marshes and lake-rims.

They may be waders, but they don't need to paddle to get a meal. Access to the ground is all they need, preferably damp ground, so they can hunt for insects and other invertebrates that they find on the surface and just beneath. Foraging is rather a business for them: they are active, preoccupied, making lots of runs and pauses, stoops and pecks. They have long legs and short beaks, like other plovers, and so they make a constant forward tilt when they peck food from the ground.

They are essentially ground birds, then, but they have the most wonderful and deeply eccentric talents in flight. They are very distinctive birds: the crest is unique, and their pattern of apparent black and white makes them stand out. In fact, when seen close up and in good light, the dark bits are a tasteful bottle-green shot with purple.

Their underwings also look very black-and-white; and when they take to the wing, this pattern flickers and strobes at you as you watch. The shape of the wing is also distinctive – very broad and rounded at the edge – and the beat is dramatically floppy. Nothing flaps quite like a lapwing. From late June to March, they prefer to be in flocks, scores

Lapwing

Where to look: *wetfields, water-edges*
When to look: *all year, in flocks in winter*
What to look for: *ragged flocks, ultra-floppy wings in flight, white bums*
What to listen for: *peewit*

and even hundreds, and the black-white-black-white wing beats, in their massed floppy-winged flights, is almost hypnotic.

Lapwings have the additional name of peewit, for their most characteristic call. Like everything else about the bird, it is remarkably distinctive. I always think of peewits as the oboes of the avian orchestra: a unique double-reed sound. They go in for all sorts of variations of the classic peewit sound, but always with the same unmistakable reediness.

Lapwings are a joy to see at any time, but if you catch them on their breeding grounds, you are in for a special treat. They split up into pairs when they breed. They are ground nesters, who will even use airfields, racecourses and golf links.

And when they court, they go for it with a very special sense of abandon. They make wild, crazy display flights. This can involve dramatic climbs, a special high-up show-off flight, followed by a wild dive to the ground. They will make daring low-level passes, like crop sprayers, then throw in a super-floppy butterfly impersonation, and, generally as a grand finish, a wig-wag, seesaw flight. This is accompanied by the wildest, most ecstatic peewitting you have ever heard: it is crazed, strident, hysterical, imploring – what lapwing could resist?

I said, when I came to the subject of magpies, that birds do not live in order to conform to human ideas about morality; well, no more do they care about conforming to human ideas of beauty and charm. But as humans – reprehensibly, as I say – find something hateful about magpies, so they – quite legitimately – find pleasure in many other species. The lapwing is unquestionably one of these: clownish, melodramatic, endearing, spectacular.

Conservation is not about saving the species we like at the expense of species we find unsympathetic. The only thing we should be trying to look after and encourage is absolutely everything: from the dullest little brown job and the most unsympathetic members of the crow and vulture tribe, right through to devastating charmers like the lapwing.

The special favourites command our attention: shouting the message that the world would be a poorer place without me and my kind. We should respond to that, and cheer the lapwing for making clear this vitally important point. And in improving the world for lapwings, we improve the world for many other different kinds of creatures. Including humans.

Pied wagtail

Where to look: *roofs, open spaces, Centre Court, Wimbledon*
When to look: *all year*
What to look for: *immensely perky, dancing little bird with wagging tail*
What to listen for: *Chiswick!, often in flight*

28. Wagtail

The Italians call them ballerinas. It is a name that suits them perfectly: wagtails are wonderfully dainty birds, and as they hawk for insects on the ground, they make a series of pas de chat, pas de loup, entrechats and fouettés, leaping into the air to beak their tiny prey.

Not that wagtail is a bad name: wagtails do indeed wag their tails, an up-and-down waggle at any time, a waggle that shows off a variegated tail and tells the world that its possessor is a wagtail and is pretty pleased about it.

The pied wagtail is the species we most often see: a dapper black and white bird that loves open space. You find pied wagtails on bare open fields in the countryside; when the vegetation gets too high, the wagtails move away. They make their living by chasing insects in these open spaces, picking them from the ground, sometimes with a dynamic little run and peck. But most characteristically, they hawk for insects in the air, jumping for them from a standing start.

They are versatile birds, a characteristic shared by most of the birds that humans regularly see, and therefore by most of the birds in this book. Any wide open space suits them, if they can find insects in it. Lawns and farmyards are fine, so are car parks and tarmac footpaths; this bird is the master of tarmac. You can bump into pied wagtails on roads, on bogs, by the coast. Pasture, ploughed fields, parkland, city parks, gardens – pied wagtails can find a way to make a living just about anywhere there is no tall and dense vegetation.

And roofs. Pied wagtails love roofs – look on a roof, see a little scuttling shape making occasional balletic leaps, and that's your pied wagtail. But if all these clues are not enough, the pied wagtail will tell you very clearly that he is who he is. Whenever he can draw breath, he will make a sweet disyllabic call: "Chiswick!" Wagtails make this call on the ground, and they make it when they fly. Their flight is a series of undulations, a little like a paper aeroplane, and is always decorated with a series of "Chiswicks".

A few years ago, a pied wagtail took a fancy to the centre court at Wimbledon, during the championships. It danced its dance right in the middle of the playing area, and constantly set off Cyclops, the device that beeps when a service is out. They are bold little birds, then, unfazed by humans, and birds of great charm as well.

There is another wagtail I should mention. The grey wagtail is a very pretty bird. Not so much grey as yellow: grey on the top, yes, but very smartly and handsomely yellow below. They are particularly associated with streams and rivers, in wooded country as well as in the open.

In the winter, when they are more buff than yellow, they will turn up alongside any kind of water, including estuaries and coasts, garden ponds and puddles on flat roofs. To continue the sporting theme, I have frequently seen grey wagtails at Sheffield Wednesday's football ground. The River Don runs round the back, in a very cheerfully untamed manner for a city river, and grey wagtails are almost always about there.

When conditions are right, grey wagtails are as confident among humans as the pied.

Wagtails are wonderfully gay and skittish.

Admittedly, all they are trying to do is find enough food to get through the day, and it's a serious and important business for them. But for we who watch them, wagtails seem to embody a kind of carefree optimism: a feeling that life is a dance and beautiful, and everything that is necessary for life can be obtained by a merry call of "Chiswick" and a few more dance steps. Life is not like that really, not for humans, and not for wagtails, but it is still deeply cheering to sight a wagtail on your roof. Another pirouette, and you walk on with the slightest spring in your step, a mite more contented with life than you were a moment before.

Seaside

29. Seagull

Seagull is a taboo word. No good birdwatcher will use it, save in jest, and no bad birdwatcher either. To say "seagull" is to say that you are not a birdwatcher at all. So, then, it is time to turn our attention to that much overlooked bird, the seagull.

My old friend Jeremy Sorensen loved the word. Sometimes, in the hides at Minsmere – which is perhaps Britain's finest nature reserve – he would grow impatient of the embarrassed cathedral hush. "Look!" Jeremy would bellow shatteringly. "A seagull!" Jeremy was head warden of Minsmere at the time.

The thing about seagulls is that there are an awful lot of them. A lot of birds, and also, a lot of species. You could, if you were scrupulously mean, cut the number of species down to maybe seven in a good British field guide. I have a rather more wide-ranging field guide on my desk right now – this one lists 26 different kinds of seagull.

And if you start to look at the pictures you find that many seagulls have an awful lot of different plumage phases. In some species, the immature gulls look very different to the adults, and in some of these, the immatures themselves vary from one year to the next. How good are you at telling a first winter herring gull from a second winter lesser black-backed gull?

My suggestion here is that we take the four commonest gulls – I think that at this stage we should abandon, if reluctantly, the term "seagull" – and concentrate on the adults. That's quite enough for starters. And I am not going to include the common gull, mainly because it is the least common of the commonly seen gulls, as well as being the least obvious.

We will begin with the black-headed gull, the bird most people think of when they hear the word "seagull". The black-headed gull is the species that says "Three quarks for muster Mark" in *Finnegans Wake*. The word "quark" was then borrowed as the name for the smallest sub-atomic particle to be

Herring gull
Where to look: *seaside, open water, rubbish-tips*
When to look: *all year*
What to look for: *pale grey back, fierce expression, yellow bill*
What to listen for: *Desert Island Discs*

isolated – Stephen Hawking's *A Brief History of Time* memorably contains a picture of "an almost free quark".

"Quark! Quark!" Black-headed gulls are noisy and numerous, and that shrill, hoarse scream is their perpetual accompaniment. They are smaller and neater than the other three frequently seen gulls, their wing beats quicker, their flight more airy and bouncy. Even when you have no clear idea of size – and size is always a problem in birdwatching – a black-headed gull is reasonably easy to pick out, at least from the other common gulls. It has a very clear white forewing against the usual gullish silver-grey – a white flash on the leading edge. That doesn't sound very obvious, I know, but it stands out pretty clearly on the actual birds.

When you see them close to, you will see that they have a red beak and red legs, again different from the other regular gulls. You will have noticed, perhaps, that I have not mentioned the black head yet. That's because the black head is a bit of a problem. It's not actually black, and anyway it isn't always there.

Let me make myself clear. The black-headed gull has a chocolate-coloured hood in the summer months. But most of the year, it has a plain white head with a dark dot behind the eye. In fact seeing a black-headed gull with his chocolate hood is one of those cheering signs of the coming spring.

They are sociable birds, and come inland. They will follow the plough and haunt rubbish tips, generally in bigger numbers than the other gulls. They fill the air with their quarks, and wheel and spin with enviable mastery of the air.

Herring gulls are the gulls that you hear on *Desert Island Discs*: the classic seagull laughing call. They are bigger than the black-headed gulls, and much fiercer to look at. They, too, come inland in the winter, and you can see them around tips and reservoirs. They have a white head, a big, distinctly vicious-looking beak, bright yellow with a red spot on it. The legs are pink. They fly with effortless grace, and they are noisy and quarrelsome. On the ground, they have a gawky, swaggering look to them. They will scavenge, and steal food from anyone who looks stealable from.

Lesser black-backed gulls are the about the same size, but where herring gulls are white and silver-grey, these are more black and white. They are black on the back as you would expect; black also on the top surface of the wings – but if you see them really well, it is clear that the black is a soft dark-grey. They are a finer, more elegant bird than the herring gull; and it is worth remembering that they have a yellow leg.

The greater black-backed gull – field guides prefer great black-backed gull – is simply huge. If you see a greater among a crowd of gulls, it is unmistakable because of its size. It's a seriously mean-looking animal: a frightening-looking beak, a tough expression and a great self-certainty about its movements. It knows it can beat up anybody that it wants to. Piracy, in the form of food-stealing, is one of its preferred ways of making a living – most birds would sooner give up food than pick a fight with a greater black-backed gull. The bird relishes its role of beach bully. They have something of the vulture about them, and in flight they are majestic, carrying that heavy body as if it weighed no more than a feather.

Often, when you see them from a distance and there are no other gulls around, you can't work out if it's a lesser black-backed gull quite close, or a greater black-backed gull a fairly long way off. Size, as I say, is a frequent point of confusion. So look at the legs – if they're pink it's a greater; and yellow or almost white denotes a lesser. A greater always looks more sharply black and white, its black back being really black. Lessers have deeper and more throaty calls than herring gulls, but greaters have the deepest and most powerful call of them all.

Seagulls are wonderfully made birds, brilliant fliers, clever and adaptable in the way they look for food, all of them with many different methods of doing so. They also seem to fly for the mere pleasure of it. Their mastery of gliding means that flight burns up very little energy, and they can stay on the wing for hours, frequently using the updraughts from cliffs to gain height. The seagull comes in many forms, and all of them somewhat special.

Black-headed gull
Where to look: *any open water*
When to look: *all year*
What to look for: *white leading edges to wings, red beak and legs*
What to listen for: *quark!*

Cormorant

Where to look: *seaside, open water*
When to look: *all year*
What to look for: *water vulture*
What to listen for: *not much*

30. Cormorant

There is something ever so slightly sinsister about cormorants. They are big black birds that look like a cross between a goose and a vulture, and they have a habit of hanging about the place looking shifty, as if they were up to something. But they are pantomime villains, not real ones. Their melodramatic bad looks are reminiscent of Hammer horror films: something you can enjoy without being in any danger of taking too seriously.

Cormorants are among the best posers of British birds. They live on fish, they are superb swimmers, diving beneath the surface in pursuit of the next meal. But they also spend a lot of time above the water drying out and, when they do so, they frequently strike dramatic, heraldic poses, wings held stiffly away from the body. It is an uncomfortable looking, almost crucifixion position, and they can hold it for hours without apparent discomfort.

Cormorants are seaside birds, but they also have a marked taste for fresh water. They can be found inland on reservoirs, lakes and rivers – and sometimes they gather in trees. They can be found anywhere where land is not too distant, and fish not too far from the surface. They have a liking for bare trees, and will assume their various, angular poses in the branches, apparently waiting for a photographer to come along.

There are more of them about than there used to be, especially on or in fresh water, because rivers are much cleaner and therefore much more full of fish; also, new gravel pits offer new opportunities for enterprising birds. They are mostly seen posing, or at work fishing. They sit on the water in a very distinctive silhouette, low in the water with the neck sticking out high and beak tilted up. They roll into the surface-dive in an easy, well-oiled motion, and will stay down for up to a minute, reaching down to ten metres below the surface.

They are fun to watch when they are busily engaged in their fishing: emerging suddenly, often a good distance from where they went down, frequently successful. They will then juggle, rather precariously, with the fish, to get it in just the right position for the important part of the whole manoeuvre: the swallow. I have seen cormorants drop fish, but that doesn't worry them too much; they just go and grab the poor thing all over again and recommence the juggle. The trick is to get the fish head first, so it will slither down smoothly without sticking in the throat. They will sometimes achieve this with a rather spirited toss in the air.

The adult birds are mostly black, with a white throat, white thigh patches in summer, and some bare yellow skin on the throat. In spring they have quiet, colourful faces and streaks of white on the head. The young birds have a rather scruffy white breast.

Cormorants are strong fliers, and will often fly very close to the surface of the sea, but they will also climb high and cross land when they have a mind to: I have seen cormorants flying over central London and fishing in the reflection of the tower of Big Ben. In flight they can look a little goose-like – especially when they are in company and form a long line. But geese never glide and cormorants never honk.

Cormorants can be effortlessly confused with their close relations, the shags. Shags are smaller (though still pretty big), slinkier, snakier, very seldom seen anywhere but on salt water, and never in trees. Breeding shags have a daft little crest on their heads. The most amusing way to try and tell them apart is to watch them fishing. Shags will often go into their dive with a jaunty little jump. They can stay under for longer, too, regularly beating a minute and a half, and times of up to four minutes have been recorded.

Cormorants are splendid birds with a rather prehistoric look about them. It is, I think, cheering that such big birds, with such specialised tastes – it has to be fish for a cormorant – can make their living in such decent numbers. There's a wildness about a cormorant that you don't find with a seagull and, for that reason, there is always something specially pleasing about the sight of one.

31. Oystercatcher

Waders can be difficult and forbidding birds to identify: long-legged brown birds, invariably seen at a vast distance, generally in large flocks that suddenly take to the skies, and weave about, and then settle again. It all seems to happen at least half a mile away, so that it is impossible to see them clearly. An encounter with a crowd of waders is the sort of thing that makes a beginning birdwatcher sigh deeply and wonder very seriously about giving up.

Here are two reasons not to give up. The first is that delight in birds is not dependent on diagnosing their species: a whirling swirling wader flock is a thrilling sight, whether they are knot or dunlin, or haven't-a-clue-but-definitely-some-sort-of-wader.

You are not on trial; you are there to enjoy yourself.

The second reason is oystercatchers. They are waders all right, and they are unmistakable. They are chunky and stocky and they have the decency not to be brownish at all. They are a strident black and white: black above and white below. And when they take to the air, they are generous enough to repeat that pattern with white wing-bars and white bums.

And if that was not enough for you to be sure, they have long, bright orange beaks. And, if you need a further clue, pink legs. They are loud, too: a clear, solid, far-carrying piping call, and they make it practically all the time. Oystercatchers are waders who insist on being identified.

They are proper seaside birds, too. Most waders like the places where humans don't care to go, and most often, they choose the tidal mudflats at river mouths, areas of soft, gooey mud that teem with small and tasty bits of life. But oystercatchers can exploit all sorts of other areas of seaside as well.

They can be seen on beaches, sand, shingle and dunes, as well as more obscure places like salt marsh and mudflats. They probe the mud with their long beaks, using that bright orange tool in a clean, vertical, downward movement. But the oyster-catchers are not restricted to that method; they also

Oystercatcher

Where to look: *shoreline, and northern fields*
When to look: *all year*
What to look for: *black and white bird,*
bright orange beak
What to listen for: *a noisy bird, loud piping*
and referee's whistle calls

forage by sight, among pebbles, and along beaches.

Oystercatchers are sociable birds, and they are generally seen feeding in loose gatherings, or roosting – resting up between meals – in tight little bands, generally all of them facing the same way. They have a heavy look about them, compared to most waders, and a deliberate, rather plodding sort of walk. When they are breeding, small groups will get together for a piping concert: hunched backs and beaks pointed downwards, they compete to make ear-splitting versions of their already strident call.

They fly well and call loudly as they fly past, most often in a small band. And they flash their black and white patterns at you in a quite shameless way. For an oystercatcher, food is generally shell-fish, and they are at home anywhere they can find it. They are not exactly relaxed about human company, unlike sparrows and pigeons, but they are a good deal more tolerant of us humans than most waders.

Oystercatchers will go inland, too, following river valleys, feeding on the banks and reaches, and they will go away from the water in search of worms, which explains why they sometimes turn up on fields, where they look rather incongruous.

Their restrainedly gaudy appearance, their love

of noise, and their burly, rather easy-going character makes them an agreeable bird to have around.
There is an air of cheery decency about oystercatchers and any bird that is so keen to be identified has
to have a lot going for it.

32. Tern

Acquire the habit of looking. That is the best advice anybody could ever have – it gives you more birds; it gives you more pleasure. If you glance at every seagull you see, you will find yourself performing a miracle, and doing so on a regular basis. For it is a fact of life that some of those seagulls are terns.

Terns are a lot like seagulls, so long as you don't look too closely. Both birds are mostly white, with some darker bits, and you often see them flying over water with bouncy, pointed white wings. And most people don't give them a second glance – oh yes, another seagull, just part of the seaside wall-paper.

I thought terns were extremely rare birds until I

Common tern

Where to look: *flying just off-shore,
fresh water, often follows rivers*
When to look: *late spring and summer*
What to look for: *elegant flight,
dramatic plunges, forked tail*
What to listen for: *sharp and rasping
calls, very unseagull-like*

got the habit of looking. Now I know that they are all around us; at least, they are in the summer, when they come here to breed. And once you start looking, you see that they are much finer than gulls, much more adroit and manoeuvrable, and altogether more dashing.

The forked tail is the giveaway, if you manage to see it. Terns have the charming nickname of sea-swallows. Most of the terns that are at all easy to see have neat little black caps – as opposed to a black head, or a black hood. And it is properly black, not chocolate-brown like the black-headed gull.

There are four or so species of tern that you can bump into at the seaside. They all have that swift, streamlined shape, and the forked tail. Their flight tends to be more rapid, less floaty than a seagull. And they are always worth keeping an eye on when they are in flight because they can put on a spectacular performance.

Terns are plunge-divers. They like to hunt by flinging themselves from a height into the sea. They are after fish, and they catch them by transforming themselves into winged daggers: sharp, pointed beak, wings folding in like the fletches on an arrow, and a headlong, utterly committed plummet at the water.

The commonest tern you will see is, oddly enough, the common tern. It has a black cap, blood-red beak with a black tip, and red legs. They are great fliers and divers, and are always a delight to set eyes on. They will come inland, too: freshwater fish taste just as good to them. Their flight is quick, but as you watch them, they will stop, turn, hover briefly and plunge. They will dive from heights of up to six metres, hitting the water with surprisingly little splash.

They nest on the ground, which makes them vulnerable, so they are always looking for safe places, secluded spots, preferably surrounded by water. For that reason, they will nest on rafts in reservoirs and lakes, when conservationists provide them. They even do so near the Thames in the middle of London; you can see terns patrolling the Thames in summer, but only if you have the habit of looking.

They are noisy, too, and, as is often the case with tremendously graceful and beautiful birds, the voice is harsh and unlovely – though splendid enough when you get used to it. It is a sound that means a tern is about and you will have the pleasure of raising your binoculars to greet him – a hard sharp, rather demanding call, quite different from any seagull: "kik!" Or maybe, "kee-rik!"

The other three terns you might bump into are worth a quick mention here. The Arctic tern is very similar to the common, but with paler wings; you are likely to bump into him on northern coasts in the summer. Sandwich terns are bigger and whiter than the rest, with black beaks and legs. Little terns are noticeably small, with a much purer white underneath. They have yellow beaks and a fast, whirring, eye-catching flight.

I am particularly keen for all bad birdwatchers to get the hang of terns. The tern is not beyond your scope: far from it. Seeing a tern is not a matter of skill, it is something that comes entirely from the habit of looking. If you look at enough gulls, you will start to see the odd tern mixed up with them. And you will have great joy, because once you have seen one, you will begin to see many. That is a wonderful lesson to learn, too, because it holds good for many different birds. Once you have seen terns, you find that quite inadvertently, you have raised your sights. You have moved from the obvious birds to the slightly less obvious. The more you look, the more you see. That rule holds good for quantity, and it also holds good for quality. Look, look, look. And when you are ready, the terns will come.

Fresh water again

33. Heron

I used to think herons were unusual birds, difficult to see, and really rather special whenever you did manage to clap eyes on one. Now, I expect you are fed up with the way I keep saying this, but – at least this time – the reason is different. I thought herons were uncommon because that's exactly what they were.

They are a lot more easy to see now than they were 30-odd years ago – not because I am a better birdwatcher, but because there are a lot more herons. The reason for that is simplicity itself: there are more fish. The more fish in a river, the more fishermen the river can support. And the reason that there are more fish is because the water is

Heron

Where to look: *water's edge , garden ponds*
When to look: *all year*
What to look for: *seriously big, long-legged bird; broad arched wings in flight*
What to listen for: *a far-carrying bark, given in flight over water*

clean, and it is now possible for a fish to live in it.

God, how the Thames used to stink. I'll never forget it; you could almost taste it. I was a member of my school boat club. I briefly, and disastrously, coxed eights, ramming a few bridges and scraping the bottom of a few boats. And I remember the stink of the Thames as it flowed through London; the great, unapologetic fetid stench of death. It spelt out the fact that nothing could live in this. And very little did; the Thames was a dead river. Now the stink has gone, and the life has returned.

That is true of the Thames, and it is true of waterways all over the country. The situation is not perfect, not by any means, but the improvement over 30 years has been spectacular. Spectacular, and blindingly obvious. You can't see the fish, but you can see the fishermen.

And herons are the most obvious of all the fishermen: huge, and often stationary, continuing their silent, remorseless hunt in full view of the passing world, so long as you don't come too close. Herons love to hunt at the edges of the water, sometimes making slow, deliberate paces, like Prince Phillip reviewing the troops; sometimes standing stockstill, staring at the water as though trying to glare a hole in it, dagger beak murderously poised, and neck muscles obviously tensed, waiting for the moment to release the killing strike.

They are tall, long-legged, and will wade thigh-deep in the water when they want to; at other times they prefer to get just their ankles wet. They are strong-looking animals, white and pale grey with a bold, black badger-stripe on the head. They have an air of concentration, of intensity, of limitless patience: that long neck like a coiled spring. At rest they exhibit a different sort of patience, often with their necks hunched and drawn in, giving themselves a silhouette like an old man waiting for the bus that never comes.

Herons can be found in shallow seawater, though they are more frequent in fresh. They are regulars on the coast of Scotland, where they have a special affinity for seaweedy rocks. They can also turn up away from water, where they look rather incongruous – sometimes standing on their own in the middle of a field for no apparent reason whatsoever. They are most often seen on their own, on their intense fishing-trips, or resting up, sometimes at the water's edge, sometimes high in a tree.

But, for all that, herons have a strong social side to them. They will often roost together in small gatherings, and they like to nest in a colony with two or three nests together, sometimes a couple of dozen. They make big, untidy, sticky nests, and the heronries are full of comings and goings, the clattering of bills and the occasional harsh, far-carrying gronk.

Herons are great fliers, and very distinctive ones. They give a clear impression of size, even at a distance, because of their slow, rhythmic wing beat and their broad, conspicuously arched wings. Their long legs stick out at the back, but when flying for any kind of distance they tuck their necks in.

If you see a big, long-legged bird flying with its neck stuck out, you might consider getting over excited: stork, crane and flamingo are all possibilities, even if the flamingo has almost certainly escaped from a collection. But really, you should consider getting over excited whenever you see a heron. Not only are they grand and impressive birds, they also send us a message: that we humans can unmake at least some of our mistakes. We have cleaned our rivers, to a fairly considerable extent, and now we have herons as a reward. Herons are signs of a better world, and that is worth a cheer. Or at least a good, loud gronk.

34. Moorhen

Black birds, sitting on the water, obviously not ducks; always looking busy, purposeful, preoccupied. They're moorhens. That is, of course, unless they are coots. Similar birds, related birds, birds with cleverly interlocking ways of making a living. And they are distinctly obliging.

They are not ducks but rails – a family that, in the main, specialises in not being seen. Rails tend to be lurkers and skulkers and lovers of thick vegetation. In fact, there is a species in South America known as the invisible rail. But these two black rails (the coots and the moorhens) are highly visible. And they are very clearly different, too. They seem mad keen to point out that, though they are both rails,

Moorhen

Where to look: *water's edge, small ponds*
When to look: *all year*
What to look for: *black bird, red forehead and beak. white flag under flicked-up tail*
What to listen for: *loud, sharp call, often from cover*

they are very different species and they don't want any confusion at all on that score. And this makes life easy for bad birdwatchers. The moorhen has a red beak with a yellow tip, and along with that a red forehead – a mark generally called a shield. The result is that your impression of the birds is strongly black and red. The coot, meanwhile, has an even more striking white beak, and even more striking white shield. The coot's head looks white from a very long way off – "bald as a coot", as the expression goes.

They are both water birds, but they each approach their watery lives in a different way. Generally speaking, the coot is out in the middle of the water and the moorhen is by the edge. The coot is more deeply committed to water, so long as it is fresh, and doesn't move too much. Lakes, reservoirs and ponds are the preferred places for both species, and the coot will also go to slow rivers.

Coots do a lot of feeding by diving from the surface, mostly to get plant materials, though they will take animals when they can get them. They don't have webbed feet – instead each big, long toe has a fringe of stiff skin around it. They will also feed on land, grazing and hunting for plant matter, and they look rather awkward and clumsy as they do so. It's not what they are best at.

Moorhens are birds of the edge. They like to be on water that is close to the plants and trees; and they like to be on land that is close to water. They forage and pick for a bigger range of food than the coot, and they take more animal stuff. They have long toes, without the coot's lobes of skin. For all that, they still swim very well, heads bobbing with determination as they do so. Coots keep their tails down on the water and look round-backed; moorhens keep their pointy tails cocked up.

Moorhens are very much at home on land, with a high-stepping, rather classy sort of walk, on greeny-yellow legs. They can climb trees too, and frequently do so to nest. They are agile and distinctive, with a cocky tail, and a busy head-bobbing action is part of their walk, as well as part of their swim. They have a narrow white stripe on their sides, which stands out surprisingly well at adistance.

Moorhens have a knack of turning up on ponds, almost as if the vegetation they like so much had given birth to them. Certainly you hardly ever see them in flight, save in a quick dash to cover. Their secret is that they prospect for likely looking foraging grounds at night, in flight.

Coots are not much seen in flight, either. They are almost always seen sitting on the water; and, in spring especially, they will go in for spectacular noisy coot-fights, when they splash and roar at each other and make a terrible din.

Coots and moorhens teach an important lesson, and they do so in a very easy way. They show us how different ways of living, different niches, can be close together but with very little overlap, and that very different species fill them. Coots and moorhens make their differences nothing less than a matter of principle. The red-billed rail and the white billed-rail have much in common, but also nothing at all to do with each other. And that is how nature works – by making lots and lots of different species to fill lots and lots of different niches.

35. Grebe

The great crested grebe is one of those birds that gets you smitten. They are easy to see, and yet somehow wholly exotic. It always seems a special privilege to clap eyes on one. A privilege, for that matter, to be sharing a planet with one.

They don't have the homely, slightly cuddly appearance of even the rarest of ducks. They are another kind of being altogether: elegant, sinuous, rather dangerous. Grebes are not related to ducks at all and, though they sit on the water, they don't do it in the same way. They are low to the surface, and long necked. They are wholly committed to a watery way of life, and hardly have anything to do with the land. They are not built for walking – their

Great crested grebe

Where to look: *lakes, reservoirs*
When to look: *all year*
What to look for: *great crest in spring and summer; silky white front*
What to listen for: *don't bother*

feet are placed far back on their bodies to give them extra heft when swimming underwater. As a result, they have the ancient nickname of arse-foot.

Grebes are at their best in spring, when both sexes acquire their great crests. Rather more than a crest – a black crown with a pair of tufts and, with it, a chestnut-and-black mane that gives them a glorious leonine appearance. They are special birds, that is clear from the first glance, and they emphasise that by disappearing every time you focus your binoculars on one. It is a fact of life that they time their dives in synchronisation with your binoculars – and they always reappear in the place you weren't looking.

But they are lovely to watch, rolling into the water with a beautifully controlled surface-dive. They are fish-eaters, and use that dangerous pointed bill to catch some impressively large fish. They will then surface, and carefully juggle the catch around, as fish-eaters must, until the fish is head down and ready to be swallowed whole. They don't dive all that deep – 2-4 metres is normal – nor do they set any records for submersion, the longest dives being around 30 seconds. The entire package is the thing that gets you – the elegance, the self-confidence, the unaffected glamour.

They shed their great crests in the winter, and

change their haunts too. In spring and summer you normally see them on shallow lakes and gravel pits; in winter they tend to go, often in flocks, to more open water – big heaving black reservoirs and sheltered coastal bays. They are pared-down, fierce-looking things in winter – grey-brown and white, and confusing, too, if you expect to see them with their crests.

But the spring and summer is when they most frequently raise your heart; they grow their lions' manes and acquire with them an almost feline expression of cunning. They are not at all shy of humans – which makes them agreeable birds for gazing on. And every so often, if you gaze enough, you will see them at their courtship, when a couple will dance across the water in a serious of ritual steps and bows – one of the finest sights in British birdwatching.

A growing interest in birds is rather like looking for stars at dusk on a frosty night. The more you look, the more you see. Where once there was a sheet of water sprinkled with ducks, there are now mallards and tufties, and two different kinds of rail (assuming you have read the previous chapter), and a cormorant too, looking black and forbidding, and there, stealing the show completely, a pair of great crested grebes, immaculate in their great and glorious crests. And the person who once saw only ducks now looks optimistically towards the grebes, and wonders if it might be the day when they perform their penguin dance – part of their courtship display really is called the penguin dance. Oh brave new world, that has such penguins in it! The birds were always there – but when you become a bad birdwatcher, the world is made new again.

36. Kingfisher

No, trust me. This is not beyond your range. I know that the kingfisher is at or near the top of the wish-list of every bad birdwatcher. I know that the bird has a slightly mythical feeling about it – so bright and beautiful that it is impossible for mere mortals to set eyes on it.

I remember, too, the incredulous delight of various bad birdwatchers of my acquaintance on seeing their first kingfisher – the almost impossible feeling of privilege. The kingfisher is a bird that bad birdwatchers don't expect to see. After all, you see pictures of it sitting by the side of a stream – a shimmering, strident, electric blue on top and sunset-salmon-pink below. So bright a bird, and yet

Kingfisher

Where to look: *hunting perches over water, low flight over water*
When to look: *all year*
What to look for: *gorgeous colours in good light, much smaller than you think, can look surprisingly drab in poor light*
What to listen for: *dramatic shrill, high call, also listen for the plop*

nobody sees it. They must be rare as albatrosses.

But they are not. All you need to see a king-fisher is a bit of luck and a bit of a knack. Plus, of course, the habit of looking. I have, on more than one occasion, seen kingfishers from the train. I gave huge delight to a reporter from Radio 3 when, as we were recording my contribution to a slightly flakey programme about Nijinksy (the ballet dancer, not the racehorse) from a hide, a kingfisher flashed – always the right word for kingfishers – into view, and I squawked my glee into the tape recorder – and the reporter's eyes shone almost as bright as the kingfisher's wing. It was a very nice moment.

Kingfishers are tiny. That's the first thing to get into your mind here. We are all familiar with the joke photograph of a a kingfisher jauntily perched on a "No Fishing" sign. But the signs are made specially for the photograph. They have to be ludi-crously small, maybe three inches long – not the sort of thing that water bailiffs stick up in real life.

For all their iridescent colours, kingfishers are hard to see when they are sitting still. And they do spend a lot of time sitting: either resting up, or fishing from a perch. Either way, they have a lot of stillness in their lives. And our eyes are better at picking out movement than stillness, however bright. The best way to see any bird is by responding to movement.

And that is how you most often see kingfishers – movement, a blue flash, low to the water, as the kingfisher flies from one perch to another. The flight is swift, and direct, and often accompanied by a piercing call, unlike any other water bird. Very often, you don't get much time – a sharp, rough squeak, a swivel of your head, a dart-like shape, a few inches above the water, disappearing on whirring wings.

That was a kingfisher. In good light, the sun catches that electric blue and makes it fizz before your eyes. On murkier days, it is more an impression of shape: tiny, dumpy, short-tailed, dagger-beak cleaving the air.

You see kingfishers on streams, smaller rivers and canals, where the current is not too swift and the water not too rocky. They like plenty of plant growth close to the edge. They will also use bigger stretches of water, but they prefer the edges and the sheltered spots. They can be seen around the coast, outside the breeding season.

They are fish specialists, as you would expect, though they will also take insects. Their way of life is based around the headlong plunge, and the underwater grab. They will dive from heights of up to 11 metres, and get as much as a metre below the surface. They are very accurate. If you are able to see one fishing, you will see him constantly bobbing his head, but they will also hover and plunge. They make a distinctive hollow plop as they hit the water, and that sound is worth listening out for – it is a clear indication that there is a kingfisher around.

They breed in a hole in a bank, which means they need steep, soft banks. That's a fairly specific demand, and it explains why you don't often see them in tamed and urbanised rivers. They are vulnerable to hard winters – they can't dive through ice, but they can regain ground with dramatic breeding performances from the survivors, when the sweet spring comes.

Kingfishers are sudden, swift and unexpected. They are what-the-hell-was-that birds. But, as you acquire the habit of looking, you learn to interpret the meagre clues of the squeak, the plop, the flash, the shape. And, with remarkable ease, you promote them from what-the-hell-was-that to bloody-hell-kingfisher. I've seen bloody-hell-kingfishers in my garden – ample reward for a lifetime of looking.

More Countryside

37. Cuckoo

Ears are as important as eyes to a birdwatcher — even a bad birdwatcher. So congratulations, you have just identified your first bird on call alone. Cuckoo! Cuckoo! It is trickier to identify this bird with your eyes, but we'll have a bash at that in a moment.

First, let's savour that huge, far-carrying, utterly unmistakable call. For a brief week or two in May, it echoes across the countryside, urgent and unstoppable. The cuckoos have flown here from Africa, and they need to breed in a hurry. It's a small window, and closing fast. And it's a desperately urgent business they have before them.

Cuckoo

Where to look: *flying over open country and parkland*
When to look: *late spring, summer*
What to look for: *hawklike silhouette*
What to listen for: *guess*

Cuckoos don't come here in vast numbers, but they are very mobile, and their huge voice makes them very effective over big areas of countryside. "Cuckoo!" It is the males that make the call, advertising themselves by means of their volume and their intensity; selling themselves as the sexiest thing around, summoning the females to mate with.

But, of course, once that happy meeting has taken place, the two happy cuckoos don't team up and play happy families. They are piratical birds who exploit the innocence of others. The females lay their eggs in the nests of small, and ludicrously naive little brown birds. In fact, a female cuckoo will sometimes be taken short, and have to get rid of her egg before she has found a host – a terrible waste of everybody's time. But that's the sort of slip-up that can happen with the cuckoo's chosen strategy.

The unlucky host, generally a dunnock, a meadow pipit, or a reed warbler, will rear the monster intruder, which will then murder its nest-mates. I never said that nature was pretty. The point of the cuckoo's strategy is that it works. There are a number of birds, all over the world, who go in for the trick of parasitising another bird's nest. But the cuckoo is the only one that does it in this country.

"The hawk never strikes when the cuckoo calls"

– an old country saying, but one based on ignorance. A cuckoo in flight is very hawk-like, with a long tail, and long, pointed wings. And a cuckoo often "cuckoos" on the wing. So the non-striking hawk is in fact a badly-seen cuckoo. It seems that wise old countrymen are often bad birdwatchers.

Cuckoos are handsome birds, dark blue-grey on the top and the chest, with a sharp break to a paler belly. You see them sometimes perched, when they will often droop their wings and flick their tails sideways, showing off large white spots. They are caterpillar specialists, though they will also take beetles. They will eat the caterpillars other birds won't touch, including the hairy ones, and the ones that carry garish colours to warn would-be predators of their unpalatability.

The female cuckoos don't say "cuckoo". You don't hear them much at all; it's the males that are the gabby ones. But when they do feel moved to speak, they make a wonderful, thrilling, rich, bubbling call.

You can find cuckoos in any kind of fairly open countryside, but the voice of the male carries so well, you can hear them in all sorts of unexpected places. This communication skill is at the heart of the way they live: they can reach out to each other from a distance, and that's how they make their daring and difficult way of life work.

38. Dunnock

The dunnock is perhaps the most overlooked bird in Britain. But it is important to get the bird straight in your mind, firstly so that you don't overlook it yourself, and secondly so that you can be perfectly sure that the dunnock is not anything else.

A growing awareness of birds is like looking at a painting of a deeply familiar place. You look at it, and it is as if you have noticed for the first time things that you see everyday. In the same way, you learn new birds, and realise that they were always there. A newly found understanding of the ambient birds gives you a new and deeper understanding of the places you always knew. Your garden, for example, or the park, or the world.

Dunnocks rather glory in being overlooked. They are at the same time common and obscure. They rejoice in skulking, secretive behaviour; and yet they are to be found all over the place: hedges, woodland – where there is plenty of ground cover – railway banking, parks, gardens, vacant lots, all kinds of semi-natural habitats. You even find them in bramble patches on cliff tops, and in little thickets high up on the moors.

They are ground feeders, and they tend to forage in the shadows and by cover. They have nothing bold, or confiding, or confident about them. They actively seek to be overlooked. Their body language isn't engaging, or cocky. They lurk about, and they tend to move in a series of creeping, shuffling movements, body low to the ground.

You can sometimes find dunnocks at the birdfeeder, but they have nothing to do with the gaudy acrobatics of the tits and finches. If you have a bush near the feeder, you will tend to find a dunnock at its foot, sneaking out diffidently to peck up the fragments that others have let fall.

The dunnock is the classical LBJ, or Little Brown Job. It is little, and brown, and that's just about it. Look more closely, and you see a greyish head, a thin beak, pale eyes, and smart but extremely understated brown and black striping on its back.

Dunnock

Where to look: *hedges, bushes*
When to look: *all year*
What to look for: *shuffling little brown job*
What to listen for: *song is a fast, flat jumble of notes, heard in winter on fine days and throughout the spring and early summer*

They are restless things when they forage, busy and hard-working, always close to cover, always unobtrusive. And as you get your eye in, you will see them very often indeed, living their discreet and preoccupied lives side by side with all the gaudier creatures that brought our attention to birds in the first place.

But I have a soft spot for dunnocks. They are cheery and indomitable little birds. They have a song that is as unexceptional – it would be cruel to say dull – as their appearance and their lifestyle. It is a rapid, flat-sounding warble, a hasty jumble of notes, cobbled together any old how, and chucked out in a rather sloppy way.

"It's not much of a song," says the dunnock, "but it's the only one I know, and I'm going to give it my best shot." And day after day, in that time when winter is barely considering turning into spring, the dunnock, being an eternal optimist, will feel moved to throw his jumble of a song into the air.

This is a good day to be writing about dunnocks. There was a heavy snowfall in the night and the world is white. But it's one of those bracing days when the sun comes with the snow, and as I write, a dunnock has been filling the air with his song for the last half-hour.

It is important to get your head around dunnocks, because they fill in the picture and because knowledge of dunnocks allows you to separate dunnocks from all the other birds that aren't dunnocks, especially sparrows. But it is also possible to love dunnocks for their own sake, for their obscurity, for the way that they make obscurity work for them as a viable way of life, and for the gameness with which they herald the coming spring. An LBJ can also make your heart lift. All birds have something of magic about them – even those that seem to have their being in dullness.

Goldfinch

Where to look: *on top of thistles*
When to look: *in open countryside, all year*
What to look for: *yellow band across black wing; black, red and white face*
What to listen for: *rattling and buzzing notes in rapid song*

39. Goldfinch

Find your weeds, and you have found your goldfinches. A patch of open ground with tall, stout weeds – that is the goldfinch's delight. They like places that have literally gone to seed. Especially when the weeds are thistles.

Such places have a slightly dismal, desolate look to us humans. That is because they were once cared for, and are now abandoned: pasture that has been overgrazed, fields that have been abandoned or set aside, open walks that no one has walked for far too long. A thistly landscape bristles with neglect. But it is a haunt of joy for goldfinches.

They are small, very agile finches, and they swoop down on such places and tease the seeds from the plant tops with great determination. Generally this is done in a decent crowd, a dozen or two, and all the time they buzz and tinkle at each other.

A group of goldfinches on the job is a busy, bright, buzzing spectacle – the air is full of movement, the flirting of those black wings, each with its vivid golden stripe, and the goldfinches' fizzing chatter to each other: noise, colour, movement, a great air of excitement and delight. "Hurray! Thistle seeds!" And they munch at them, relishing them most in their moist and milky state.

Goldfinches also have a passion for teasels – those spiky, fist-sized seed heads that people spray gold for table decorations. Goldfinches prefer theirs natural and unadorned. They hang from the swaying tops, and work away with their beaks, in order to defeat the plant's finest and spikiest defence mechanisms, and get to the sweet, milky seeds beneath.

A charm of goldfinches – that's the old collective noun, and why not? Goldfinches seem specially sent to give delight to humans. They are improbably gaudy, with that bright, almost clown-like head, a bright red face, set off dramatically with long white sideburns and a black nape. They are not discreet birds.

The pleasure goldfinches give to humans has also been their downfall. For wild creatures, a human liking is every bit as dangerous as a human disliking.

Goldfinches in cages were all the rage in the 18th and 19th centuries; the trade in them made serious inroads into the wild population. But they are tough and resilient birds, and when the persecutions stopped, the birds bounced back.

Goldfinches have a wider diet than seeds, taking insects and other small creatures in the spring, when there aren't so many seeds about. But seeds are what they are best at, with their acrobatic talents and their tough, finch's beaks, a tool that is beautifully designed for dealing with seeds.

Goldfinches will come to bird-feeders, where they show they are almost as acrobatic as tits, despite their bigger size. This is a recent behavioural change, and it probably comes down to the use of niger seed in wild bird mixes. From a close look, they can seem impossibly loud and showy – yet when you see a flock all absorbed in feeding, the tawny, sandy background colour is the thing that dominates. That's until they take to the wing again, and fill the air with their noise, their colour, and their exuberance in an airy, bouncing, almost weightless flight. Goldfinches seem to get a great buzz out of life – from kicking up a racket and flaunting their bold colours, from eating those milky seeds, and, above all, from being all goldfinches together. A charmed life, perhaps.

40. Yellowhammer

We regularly lavish praise on the perfection of our fellow-creatures, and especially on the miraculous adaptations that allow them to survive – from the cheetah's speed to the humming-bird's wing. And it's all fair enough, as anyone who has seen a charging cheetah, or a backwards-flying humming-bird, will agree.

I have also, at various points in this book, written very positively about the way Britain's obvious birds are often highly adaptable in their behaviour: they can change their diet and their way of life in order to exploit opportunities provided by humans. I have praised pigeons and starlings, among many others, in these pages.

Yellowhammer

Where to look: *on high perches in spring*
When to look: *around open country all year*
What to look for: *yellow head, white edges to tail*
What to listen for: *a-little-bit-of-bread-and-no -
cheeeeeeeese*

But we don't give much thought to the question of luck. Luck has played an absolutely colossal part in shaping the planet, and the creatures that live on it. The old story, taught in schools 50 years ago, was that the dinosaurs were stupid lumberers, defeated by the smart, swift little mammals. And it's not true at all. Dinosaurs ruled the earth very capably for 100 million years, which is a target human beings will struggle to reach.

Their time was ended not by their stupidity, but by a meteor, which struck the earth like a million atom bombs. The creatures that survived were skulking, furtive, and lucky. These included the mammals. Without the luck of that meteor, the mammals would have stayed furtive – they would never have dominated the earth.

The biggest crisis to hit the planet, since that 65-million-year-old meteor, is the rise of humankind. Humans have changed the earth every bit as dramatically as that meteor. And, often, the creatures that survive in changing conditions just happen to have the right kind of luck.

That, in a small way, is the story of the yellowhammer. The yellowhammer is the bird of farmland. It is the one that sings "a-little-bit-of-bread-and-no-cheese". The males have bright yellow heads and fronts, and they like to take a high, dominant place – a songpost – and sing their hearts out in the spring.

They like open fields, heaths, commons, bushy hillsides. They like a mixture of open ground and high song posts, with some low vegetation. And these, as it happens, are precisely the conditions that humans have created again and again, across lowland Britain. We call them farms: open fields to forage on, hedges to hide in, telegraph poles to sing from.

Yellowhammers are quite fussy birds. They don't like an environment that is too open, and they don't like one that is too closed. Time and again, a farm is just right. And so yellowhammers haunt farmland, not because they are clever, or brilliant, or remarkable, but because they are lucky. It has to be said, though, that they are not as lucky as they used to be. There are far fewer seed-bearing plants to be found on farmland these days. Perhaps the yellowhammer's luck is beginning to run out.

They are very nice birds as well – so perhaps it's the humans that are lucky. But that "little-bit-of-bread-and-no-cheese" mnemonic can be confusing. The main body of their song is a musical, lilting, rattle. It is followed, when the bird is in the mood, with a drawn-out final note – that's the "cheeeeeese". But the yellowhammer will only serve up the "cheese" when he thinks it appropriate. And when he is feeling particularly inspired, he will serve up a double portion: "cheeeese-cheeeese".

Look around when you hear the song, it pays to look high: telegraph posts and wires, treetops. And, in good light, the sight is especially rewarding – a boldly-coloured bird: bright yellow head and front, ginger breast-band. The female is drab and difficult to pick out, but the male is easy. Flashing his head, singing his song with or without cheese, and generally celebrating his luck.

41. Buzzard

It is amazing that we still have buzzards. Humans have worked, both on purpose and by accident, to drive them to extinction. But impossibly, the buzzards have held on. Now, in vast parts of the country, they prosper.

Buzzards are birds of prey – big, burly and unapologetic. They perch, large and threatening, or they soar, with insolent ease. And they have, in not much more than 30 years, gone from being a very rare sight to, in many places, a pretty common one.

From the 18th century to the present day, buzzards have been shot and poisoned, mainly to protect pheasants. The fact that buzzards infinitely prefer rabbits has nothing to do with it – they are

Buzzard

Where to look: *sky, especially over open country*
When to look: *all year*
What to look for: *big, chunky gliding bird with patterned wings*
What to listen for: *very noisy for a bird of prey; shrill, ringing, sky-filling cries*

birds of prey, so, by gamekeepers' logic, they have to go. And the fact that the persecution of buzzards is now illegal has not stopped it, either.

As if that were not bad enough, the buzzards were then walloped by the myxomatosis outbreak of the 1950s – kill the rabbits and the buzzards starve. After that, they were clobbered by the problem of pesticides entering the food chain. This caused the problem of eggshell-thinning in birds of prey. Buzzards, like all other birds of prey, were unable to breed successfully.

But the buzzards hung on somehow, in the remoter and wilder places of the far west, and now, in many places, they prosper. Look for the big, raggedy silhouette: wide wings, a wide tail often held in a fan, that air of easy self-confidence as they ride the air. You hear them, too, for they are gabby birds: a shrill, far-carrying mewling sound, often in two marked syllables.

A number of things have been working in their favour. The dangerous pesticides are now illegal in this country – though DDT is still manufactured, and is widely used in the third world because it is cheap. The rabbit population is now booming. And persecution is at a much lower level than it was before the war.

This is not because gamekeepers are more

enlightened; there are just much fewer of them about the place. You will find buzzards all over the west side of the country. They are seen more frequently in the south-east these days, but they are still pretty exceptional in the east.

There are a number of possible reasons for this: the first is that efficient, and illegal, gamekeepering is holding the buzzards back at the borders of their range. But nothing is ever straightforward with wildlife. Buzzards show a strong inclination to breed in the places they themselves were brought up. And it is also highly likely that the rabbit increase means that the ancestral buzzard lands can now hold more buzzards. Certainly in the west country, you can see buzzards in impressive numbers – 50 or more together at a winter roost is by no means unusual.

The future pattern is hard to predict, but it is possible that buzzards will eventually burst the banks of their current range, and spread out eastwards into the forbidden lands. Buzzards certainly represent a success story, and if that is the sort of thing that only excites game-shooting people to start demanding a legal cull, it means that those of us who don't need to kill birds have more birds to enjoy.

And buzzards, common or not, are splendidly

dramatic. They will take carrion when it is about, but they are mostly hunters. They use the perch-and-glare technique, scanning the countryside from a good look-out, ready to glide carefully down on anything they spot. Or they will hunt on the wing, using their nonchalant soar to cover the ground. In direct flight, they look heavy and clumsy – it is the gliding and soaring at which they show their mastery. They can hover, too, generally into a stiff breeze, but they are not spectacularly good at it, compared to kestrels. They will even hunt on the ground, walking through the right sort of areas, like a terrible avenger.

It is always good to see a buzzard. I remember the thrill of my first pair of buzzards as a boy bird-er: the impossible luck of it, the impossible grace of them. Now you can see buzzards all the time; and that, for my money, makes the pleasure still richer – soaring high, unconquered.

42. Willow warbler

You will have noticed that, as this book progresses, I am bringing in slightly more difficult birds. I am, it is true, trying to encourage the bad birdwatcher to raise his sights. I hope I am not pushing you too far by writing about the willow warbler, one of those little greeny-olivey birds that take up so much room at the back of good field guides.

All those little birds look more or less the same, and the problems of trying to tell a willow warbler from a chiffchaff seem to be insuperable. Generally, in these field guides, the pictures are on opposite pages. They might be the same bird; and these pictures have been specially drawn to show off what differences there are.

Willow warbler

Where to look: *scrub and bushes*
When to look: *late spring, summer*
What to look for: *drab little greeny bird, slim beak*
What to listen for: *sweet, sweet, song descending the scale*

Never mind. Help is at hand. When you want to tell a willow warbler from a chiffchaff, just get a good close look, and it is obvious. The head is a slightly different shape; the willow warbler's tail is ever so slightly longer; but the real give away is the tertials, and the primary projection.

And, if you can't tell a willow warbler from a chiffchaff after that, then there must be something wrong with you. I've got it right, you know: the long yellowy-brown feathers on the edge of the wing are longer in the willow warbler than in the chiffchaff, and so are the greeny feathers towards the middle of the wing.

I have to confess, I have never noticed such things on any living bird. If I had a dead bird of each species in my hand, I might, at a pinch, be able to see what all this stuff is about. But when it comes to telling the species apart, in the field, from a quick glimpse, I am hopeless. This is a book written for bad birdwatchers by a bad birdwatcher; let's have no mistake on that score.

And yet, I am including these two birds in this book because they *are* easy to tell apart. And if you get the trick, you will have incomparable joy doing it: partly for the pleasure of being able to perform the trick, and partly because of the delight the birds will bring you.

I want you to tell birds like these apart by their voices. It's not actually the hardest thing in the world. In these pages, you have already read about tawny owls and cuckoos – two birds which you will already know by call, and which you will readily identify by their voices. All I am looking for here is a chance to escalate.

These two little birds, willow warbler and chiffchaff, are very similar, and yet they form a linked pair of opposites. Both are warblers; both are migrants. The chiffchaff flies to southern Europe, and northern Africa – a few even brave our winters. And they are among the first migrants to return to this country when the spring comes. It is a special day when you hear the first chiffchaff of the year – generally in late March.

And it is an easy song to understand; the chiffchaff says its name. The Germans call the chiffchaff a zilpzalp, which is even better. It is possible to confuse a chiffchaff with a great tit, which fills the air of early spring with a brassy "teacher, teacher, teacher". But the chiffchaff gives an equal weight to each syllable, rather than a heavy stress on the first. And it doesn't produce notes in strict pairs. More often, it presents a sequence: "chiff chaff chiff chaff chaff chaff chiff chiff, etc, etc".

The willow warbler comes later – in the last

week or two of April. The best thing, if you don't have a friend to point out the bird for you, is to buy a tape or a CD. There's an address at the back of the book, if you want to follow this up. But I'll have a go at describing the song.

I'll have a go, because it is perhaps the single best moment in the birdwatching year, the moment when you hear for the first time that simple, lisping descent of the scale. These ridiculous tiny creatures – you could put a couple of dozen into your hat – have flown all the way from eastern Africa, on wings that are absurdly small, despite the primary projections and the tertials. They have come all this way to be with us, to celebrate the spring with us, and to breed and raise their family among us. How can we not rejoice at that?

Chiffchaffs like tall, mature trees, and will come into parks, and commons, and gardens. Willow warblers need bigger open spaces, and scrubby bushes, but they can be found on urban commons, so long as these have not been too severely tamed.

Listen. That is the final message as I move onto the last section of this book. Learn to listen, and there will be so many more birds in your life. And, if you can bring in the willow warbler, then you will have a more profound joy in the coming spring than ever you experienced before.

Pilgrimage birds

43. Avocet

You, too, can see special birds. You, too, can set eyes on the most dramatic and beautiful and extraordinary birds that have ever flapped a wing over this country. You don't have to be a brilliant birdwatcher; you don't need colossal skills; you don't need state-of-the-art equipment. All you need to do is travel a bit. And to the right places.

Is it hard to see York Minster? All you need to do is to go to York, and you find yourself gazing on the soaring stone. So, I am closing this book by offering you a series of pilgrimages: to the glorious, and protected, and managed, places that are among the cathedrals of wild Britain. If you go there at the right time – and I will tell you the right time – then

Avocet

Where to look: *brackish lagoons, estuaries in winter, all RSPB literature, also RSPB ties*

When to look: *all year, but they abandon certain breeding grounds in autumn and early winter*

What to look for: *elegant black and white bird, turny-uppy beak*

What to listen for: *says its Dutch name: kluut!*

you will almost certainly encounter the greatest treasures of British life.

And we will start with the avocet. That is, of course, a hint: the avocet is the logo of the Royal Society for the Protection of Birds, and the RSPB owns, and runs, most of the aforementioned cathedrals – and all eight of the pilgrimage birds I will describe for you can be seen on RSPB reserves. Entry to these places is free to members. So join. And if, by chance, you haven't joined by the time you make your pilgrimage, then you can sign up on the spot and enter free. And then go on your next pilgrimage to your next cathedral, also free.

The avocet is wonderfully special. It went extinct as a breeding bird in this country. But, as chance would have it, in the Second World War there were areas along the coast of East Anglia that were neglected, abandoned, used for tank practice, or flooded for defence purposes. And, as luck (remember luck?) would have it, these places turned out to be wonderfully suitable for avocets.

And so the avocets came back, recolonising from Holland, and they found that the chance-created brackish lagoons were just perfect for them. So naturally – the right word if ever there was one – they started to breed again. At first this was a great secret, and for years the places where avocets bred were strictly looked after. And very few people were allowed to see them.

But these days, all that is changed. Minsmere, in Suffolk, is a place that heaves and hums with visitors. It is a honeypot for birdwatchers of the bad kind, as well as the good. The hides there are full of people trying to tell a mallard from a tufty.

And they are there to enjoy the glorious experience of bad birdwatching, and to set eyes on the avocets: birds that were extinct, birds that were almost mythical, birds that absolutely anyone can now roll up and revel in. I laughed out loud the first time I went into a Minsmere hide: how absurd to see a bird I had thought I would never be able to clap eyes on – and such a lot of them. It was, as I have said many times, as if I were looking out on a field of unicorns.

They are gorgeous things to watch: black and white, leggy, that absurd turny-uppy beak, which they use for sieving and scything through the water in search of small bits of life, shrimps being a favourite. They like to be in numbers, too. They come to Minsmere in great crowds in order to breed. And they can be found gathered together in river estuaries across the country, when not breeding.

The Exe estuary is a good place to to catch them. But the best place to go is Minsmere, and, in particular, to the hides around a man-made system of lagoons that is prosaically called The Scrape. The avocets are there from mid-February through to the early autumn: busy, preoccupied, quarrelsome, affectionate and endlessly elegant. In March, you will see them court and mate: the male on top of the female, with a brief flourish of wings that turns him into an archangel, before he drops to one side, momentarily leaving one wing draped over his mate.

And as you watch the avocets, and revel in their elegant joys, and battles, and preoccupations, you can say to yourself, gloatingly, "and they were once extinct". Extinct, anyway, as breeding birds in this country. And that adds a special joy. Life is infinitely fragile, but with luck, and hard work, and money, and serious human will, life can be cherished. And life can go on.

Osprey

Where to look: *Scottish lochs, Lake District*
When to look: *all year, but most easily found at known breeding sites in spring and summer*
What to look for: *if a bird of prey plunges into the water, it's an osprey; black and white face*
What to listen for: *loud whistling around nest*

44. Osprey

Years ago, the conservation organisations that ran nature reserves held to the theory that people were a very bad thing. The location of rare birds was kept secret, so that people wouldn't disturb them, steal their eggs and generally make a nuisance of themselves.

These days, conservation organisations across the world take the exact opposite view. The great wildlife sites are no longer no-go areas. The spectacular, and sometimes very rare, creatures that live in them are at home to visitors. They are available to us all; even – or perhaps especially – to bad birdwatchers. Where visitors were once kept out, they are now positively solicited.

The osprey is another species that went extinct as breeding birds in this country. They were persecuted by those who thought the ospreys were stealing all their fish, and they were also shot by collectors. People were, indeed, a bad thing. But then one pair of ospreys came back and started to breed in Scotland, to great fanfares and celebrations, in 1955. The location of their nest was kept secret – intrepid egg-collectors came up against even more intrepid guards. Wildlife conservation became a kind of siege. Yet the eggs were still sometimes stolen, the nest tree was cut through, and even set on fire, and once the visitors' centre was burned down.

It is shockingly different these days. If you go to Loch Garten – that's the secret place, you can read about it in guidebooks and on the RSPB website – you will be welcomed with open arms. You will be able to climb to a viewing platform, and observe the ospreys on the nest. You can also watch them on a television screen: a camera is mounted by the nest site, and it relays the images to the many pilgrims who come to gaze. RSPB staff are on hand to talk about ospreys, or any other birdwatching matter that is on your mind.

And they will tell you that, slowly, ospreys are spreading again – recolonising their old haunts. In one or two places, they have been deliberately rein-troduced. You can even find them in England: at Rutland Water, and at Bassenthwaite, in Cumbria. A pair recently bred in Wales for the first time on record.

Ospreys are worth making a fuss off. They are birds of prey, and their prey is fish. They live by large open bodies of water, and they hunt on the wing. And they make their living by plunging talons-first into the water, and grabbing fish with grappling-iron feet.

It is an astonishing and dramatic technique. They don't go deep, no more than a metre, but their descent is staggering: the final strike made with half-closed wings, the feet swinging forward for the grab at the last moment. They will make their plummet from as much as 70 metres, though 25-30 metres is more usual. They will also drop in from as little as five metres.

Ospreys often make their descent in a series of stops: checking that the fish they have picked out is still available, adjusting if it has moved, but is still close enough to the surface to be taloned. After a successful plunge, they will carry the fish to a perch or to the nest, generally with the fish head first, which is more aerodynamically efficient.

Ospreys spend the winter in Africa, and fly back

in the spring. In spring and autumn they can turn up unexpectedly at all sorts of watery places, inland, and on the coast, where they sometimes hang around for a few days, refuelling for the next leg of the journey.

They look strongly black and white, with a noticeable kink in the leading edge of the wing. Sometimes they pinch in the wingtips, when their lazy, intermittently gliding flight can look rather gull-like. They make a bold picture when perched: dark body and pronouncedly white head, marked with a dashing black streak.

But it is in action that the ospreys are best seen, and Loch Garten provides the perfect opportunity. The birds are long accustomed to their fame, and visitors don't worry them at all. That is as it should be, I think. Conservation will only work if humans want the wild life, and the wild places. The best advertisement for the conservation of birds is — well, birds.

The public ospreys of Loch Garten trumpet out the message: that birds are wonderful and thrilling and they belong to us all. To an extent anyway. As you see them soar and plunge, you will thrill to the fact that they belong, most of all, to themselves.

45. Bewick's swan

There is nothing quite like a swanfall. It is one of the most thunderous and dramatic events in the birdwatching year; and you can watch it from the comfort of a centrally-heated viewing station. You can't say that conservation organisations don't make things easy for bad birdwatchers.

The Bewick's swan is one of those other two swans already mentioned in these pages, in the chapter that mostly concerned the mute swan. That's the normal swan; but there are also the two swans that you don't see every day. Bewick's swans breed in Siberia, and come here for the winter, and they are available for bad birdwatchers, at known locations, from mid-October to March. The most luxurious of these, and the easiest one for swan viewing, is at Slimbridge, in Gloucestershire, the headquarters of the Wildfowl & Wetland Trust.

At the Trust, they are so keen to make things easy for both birds and birdwatchers, they even feed the swans, chucking out bucketfuls of spuds and grain at specified times of the day. Some conservationists think this is less than ideal, creating an essentially unnatural situation, with birds in unnatural concentrations. As for the birds themselves, they eat the spuds, and don't trouble their heads with the ethics.

They are gloriously handsome birds – pure white, black and yellow on the bill. They are the smallest of the three British swans, and are the most goose-like: neck straight, unlike the traditional S-shape of the mute swan's neck.

And they are but absolutely nuts about dominance. Bewick's swans winter in pretty close proximity, spuds or no spuds, and it is essential, for their wellbeing, that they work out who gives way to whom. They operate in family units, male and female, with the year's crop of youngsters, which are browny-grey about the head and neck. And, while the Bewick's swans may be the smallest swans, that doesn't exactly make them small.

No: they are huge, and they state their claim

Bewick's swan

Where to look: *certain inland waters, potato fields*
When to look: *late autumn and winter*
What to look for: *swan with a straight, chunky neck*
What to listen for: *bugle calls*

to a decent place in the dominance hierarchy by swimming at each other, in great threatening gang-handed family groups, rocking their necks back and forward in unison, and bugling at each other. It is a glorious, strident sound and, in this context, is a military call to action. It all adds up to a wonderfully impressive sight, and sound. Smaller families back down to bigger ones; and in this way, the most successful summer breeders set themselves up to become the most successful winter survivors. It is not about fighting, it is all about threat: numbers, size, sound.

When the swans arrive at a winter location, it is called a swanfall, and the first duty of the newly arrived swans is to establish their credentials: as near to boss family as they deserve, as near to boss family as they can. And so they swim, and they bugle, and they neck at each other. They are seeking above all to be impressive. And no human can doubt that they succeed. Handsomely.

Bewick's swans can be found in other places; the easiest are the Ouse, and the Nene Washes, in Cambridgeshire. But Slimbridge makes it all astonishingly easy. You may object that it feels a little tame, but the birds themselves have commuted all the way from Siberia, and they don't think of their lives as a soft option. Best enjoy the birds, as the birds enjoy their spuds.

Incidentally, the Bewick's swan is the only bird in this book to be named for a human. Many birds in the world are named for human beings, and there is often a story attached: Francois le Vaillant named the Narina Trogon for his famously beautiful mistress from the Khoi Khoi tribe, and Klaas's cuckoo for his Khoi Khoi manservant. Thomas Bewick was an English engraver and ornithologist of the 18th century, and a pioneer of the study of birds. It is right that such a fine bird should be named after him.

The Bewick's swan is bird of great drama. They are very faithful to their wintering places, which explains why you don't see them in your local park. But they are there for the pilgrims to revel in, and they enlarge the visitor's understanding of the possibilities of birds, and birdwatching.

Marsh harrier

Where to look: *over reedbeds*
When to look: *some birds stay all year, but easiest to see spring and summer*
What to look for: *big bird gliding over reeds, wings in a shallow vee*
What to listen for: *mostly silent, but makes mad screaming noises in courting sky dances*

46. Marsh harrier

Speed isn't everything. Slowness also has its virtues. We like to think that birds of prey are creatures defined by extreme speed. Some are – and we will get to them before the end of the book – but there are birds of prey whose essential strategy is based on extreme lack of speed.

The marsh harrier was once down to a single nesting pair. Persecution, and the draining of marshes, were the main reasons for their scarcity, and their recovery was made next to impossible by pesticides. This problem has affected all birds of prey, as previously discussed in these pages.

I remember my shock when I first saw one – over a damp field on the edge of the Norfolk

Broads. Flying, yes, impossibly slowly. And utterly distinctive, with the wings held in a sharp vee: a dihedral, as a student of aerodynamics would say.

Students of aerodynamics will know how hard it is to get an aircraft to fly very slowly. Below a certain speed, an aircraft simply falls out of the sky. A stall, it is called. You can demonstrate that for yourself with a paper aeroplane: it will glide, slow down, and then nosedive. A good paper plane will pick up speed in the dive, and glide again. The difficulty of flying slowly is what makes landing the trickiest part of a pilot's life.

A marsh harrier operates at an extreme lack of pace, which is as difficult a trick to perform as the flat-out pace of a falcon. Quartering – that's the right word. A marsh harrier quarters the ground – above reedbeds and fields, wings held high, keeping immaculate control, a control which always seems precariously balanced on the very edge of a stall.

From this calm, dignified flight, they drop, with quiet precision, onto the creatures below: voles and other rodents, birds including ducks. In the breeding season they will take young birds, including gulls, from their nests.

The females are dark with creamy heads, the males an extravagant mixture of rather subtle tones – tricoloured in pale grey and copper, with black wing-tips. They migrate south in the winter, or at least that's what they are supposed to do; these days, with our milder winters, increasing numbers are staying around all year.

Marsh harriers have been a great conservation success story over recent years. The pesticides are now illegal, and reedbeds – essential places for marsh harriers – are very carefully managed by conservation organisations. As a result, these birds are not at all hard to see. The easiest place is Minsmere, in Suffolk, but they can also be seen at Leighton Moss, in Lancashire, and Titchwell, in Norfolk. There are also other places listed on the RSPB website.

Minsmere is the easiest, no doubt about that. The marsh harriers love the acres of reedbed and there are several nests there each season. Sometimes, one dominant male will lord it over two, or even three nests, each with its attendant female.

If you are about in early spring, you might just catch one of the finest sights in British birdwatching: the skydance of the marsh harrier. This is a courtship ritual, it often takes place at extreme heights, with an awful lot of screaming – male and female spiralling, sometimes passing food to each other, sometimes tumbling through the air with their talons locked together: a wild and deeply thrilling experience.

But you are more likely to see them at their silent quartering, that slow, ultra-confident flight, often fairly low over the ground, or over the tops of the reeds. In moments like this, especially at Minsmere, you get the feeling of a world almost exploding with life, a place rich in every kind of creature, and you would not be surprised at anything that turned up; and, always around, the noise, and bustle, and excitement, of life going on: birds breeding, moving, feeding, resting, surviving. It seems as if the most extraordinary things are a matter of routine, and the heaving nature of life is simply inevitable. There will be one more reason for a Minsmere pilgrimage before this book is quite over.

47. Gannet

Are hunting gannets the most spectacular sight in British wildlife? There are a number of contenders for this, and we have now reached the stage of the book when we are meeting one in every chapter. But *BBC Wildlife* magazine put gannets as number one. You couldn't argue with it, either.

Gannets are perhaps the craziest hunters of all. Huge white birds, with yellow heads, black wingtips, and the most extravagant dagger beak you have ever seen. They have set-in-front eyes that both glare forwards, to give them the greater accuracy of binocular vision. They are dashing, active fliers, with a powerful wing beat.

They patrol the seas at about 30 metres up, and

when they see something that they fancy, they fold their wings and simply fling themselves at it. When there is a shoal of fish, the gannets gather in numbers, and carpet-bomb the area, using themselves as the bombs.

It seems the most ridiculous way of hunting ever devised: to see something, and to go for it, without an atom of restraint. But it works, and gannets prosper as a result. They are seabirds, which is quite different from being a bird of the seaside. Gannets are birds of the open ocean and, for most of the year, that's where they are – out on the water or in the air above it; fishing or resting.

The snag for a birdwatcher is that seabirds are mostly at sea, while birdwatchers are mostly on land. But seabirds can't build their nests on the sea. They need a bit of land for that. In particular, they need a bit of land that is safe from rats, and other eggs thieves, and also safe from human interference. And, mostly, that means rocky islands, preferably uninhabitable outcrops sticking out of the sea, the places where no one but a lunatic would ever go.

Very obligingly, there is one spot on mainland Britain where the gannets come to nest. And human pilgrims can watch them there in comfort.

That is Bempton, in south Yorkshire – three

Gannet

Where to look: *out at sea, nesting colonies*
When to look: *all year, but at colonies,*
spring and summer
What to look for: *massive white bird*
plunging dementedly from a dizzy height
What to listen for: *silent except in colonies*

miles of cliffs where you can see not only gannets but also puffins, guillemots, razorbills, kittiwakes and fulmars. And you might also see seals and dolphins. This is a rather special place.

The show is available from April to mid-August, with the gannets staying on into September: a spectacular sight, a spectacular sound and, perhaps most of all, a spectacular smell. Birds come to these dizzying cliffs in colossal numbers, and the human pilgrims who come to see them do not disturb them for an instant.

Gannets are wonderfully dignified and purposeful when flying at full speed: complete masters of the air. But they have difficulties at very low speed. We discussed the problem of stalling in the last chapter. Gannets come to the nesting site, drop speed at the last moment, and then stall out of the sky. But it is not an altogether controlled movement, and it is not unusual to see a gannet fall flat on his face at the moment of landing. But they don't lose their dignity for long, for they are deeply impressive things, with black, Alice Cooper make-up around the eyes that gives a particularly fearsome expression.

There is a strange sense of privilege in seeing seabirds in these numbers. Mostly, they turn up on the coast at odd times, when blown in by gales, in small groups or as singletons – chance-seen birds, and always a delight. I remember, in particular, a group of a dozen or so gannets fishing close to the shore in Cornwall. I had walked into a small town to spend the night; the gannets were there as a welcome, and they were there throughout the evening – I saw them as I left my B & B to find a pub, and I saw them last thing from the pub window as the sky darkened, still hard at it.

But, at Bempton, they are there in numbers. Bempton is their New York – a seabird metropolis. And it is a corner of the world that is shockingly easy to get to, and at the same time shockingly wild.

Red kite

Where to look: *skies in Wales and over the M40; pub carparks in the Chilterns*
When to look: *all year*
What to look for: *a bird of prey with long slim wings and tail, tail deeply notched, used as a rudder*
What to listen for: *loud, ringing squeal*

48. Red kite

It's another bird of prey, it's another bird that got severely hammered in this country, and it's another pilgrimage bird. None of this is coincidence. Birds of prey have had it tougher than any other kind. They always do. And they are the most spectacular birds to look at – which is just another of the disadvantages they have suffered.

They may be the toughest birds when it comes to killing things but, when it comes to surviving, they have the hardest job. No place can hold very many predators. There are always far, far more wildebeest than there are lions; there are always far, far more blue tits than there are sparrowhawks. A bird of prey is by definition rare, rarer than the creatures it preys on, at the very least.

Birds of prey are spectacular. They get noticed when they are about. And, for that reason, they have been persecuted since the invention of the shotgun. They have been shot because they might interfere with the human pleasure of shooting other birds – whether the birds of prey actually kill and eat such birds or not.

But birds of prey are noticeable, and threatening, and that has made them an affront to gamekeepers, and the owners of shoots. Birds of prey have always been a target; they have had it hard for centuries.

Masses of work from conservation organisations like the RSPB, and the outlawing of certain pesticides, have helped their recovery. Birds of prey have been looked after, their places protected, their nests guarded. And, in some cases, birds of prey have been deliberately reintroduced. And it has worked: once-vanished birds of prey are now back in their former haunts. This is true of the white-tailed sea eagle, and it is spectacularly true with the runaway success of the red kite.

The red kite was once a common sight in London. Hamlet – admittedly a Dane, but his author knew London better than Copenhagen – says, when he considers murdering of his uncle:

I should have fatted all the region kites
With this slave's offal.

The red kite may no longer be a common sight in London, but it is a common site on the M40, where the road passes the great escarpment of the Chilterns – a fact that renders the road particularly perilous for bad birdwatchers – and good ones, too.

For a red kite is a must-watch bird, an un-look-awayable bird: long, narrow, kinked wings and a deeply forked tail, which it bends and twists as a rudder. It is most conspicuous from below, not for its redness, but for the large pale patch on its wing. But that twisting, forked tail makes the bird unmistakable.

The best place to see red kites, when travelling at less than 70 mph, is Gigrin Farm in Wales – half a mile south of Rhayader in Powys. You can also see them over pub carparks in the Chilterns, and from the RSPB's Black Isle visitors' centre, near Inverness. They are also easy to see at other sites dotted around the country, where they are gradually spreading out from their centres of reintroduction: Rockingham in the Midlands, the Dumfries and Galloway Trail in south-west Scotland. The Welsh kites are, if you like, the real ones: ancestors of the birds that survived when all the others were wiped out. But seeing the introduced birds, and their own descendants, has a different kind of thrill – a good feeling that human intervention is not always bad news for a bird.

They are gorgeous birds to see, flying with a supreme gliding nonchalance. Birds of prey need to be masters of what they do; they have chosen a very hard way to make a living, and if they were to slip below excellence, the job couldn't be done.

Kites are renowned for eating carrion, but that's not the soft option it seems to be. It still requires consummate aeronautical skill. Kites hunt for dead meat by soaring high, and airy, and confident, with acute eyes scanning the ground beneath. They also kill a fair amount for themselves, taking rats, voles, rabbits, and birds, especially young birds on the nest.

Most of the time, when you look at birds, you have to think of humans as the most frightful villains, and that can get really rather depressing. But, when you look at red kites in Britain, you can heave a sigh of self-satisfaction, and think about how good humans are, what fine things humans have done for their birds. It was human intervention that brought the red kites back to us. Now, in the right places – increasingly large places, too – they are almost common birds. Humans *can* do things right, when we put our minds to it. Admittedly, humans caused the trouble in the first place, but there's no profit in meditating on that. Observe the kite, and think: "Well, that's at least one thing we've got right." It's worth making the pilgrimage for that thought alone.

49. Bittern

Well, you may not see this one. They are not birds that like to be seen. They are the keepers of a secret: they are lurkers, and sneakers, in the most secret places in the country. But go there at the right time, and you can hear them. Go there in late April and May, and you have a very high chance indeed of hearing the most peculiar bird sound in the world.

They call it booming, but that's not entirely right, it sounds altogether too explosive. Their scientific name, *Botaurus*, calls in both oxen and bulls, evoking a kind of strangled, roaring moo. But that's not entirely right, either. The boom of the bittern combines a humming, with the hollowness you get from blowing over the top of a bottle, all

Bittern

Where to look: reedbeds

When to look: all year, but most noticeable in spring

What to look for: a huge brown owl-like bird flying over reeds

What to listen for: the famous bittern boom, in spring, even at night: a deep wooomp mixed in with a kind of swallow.

That's not so clear either, is it? The best answer is to go and hear it for yourself. Especially, to go and hear it at dawn on a May morning, when there is a ghostly blanket of mist over the reedbeds, because that's where bitterns like to be. If you get into a reedbed, and get your head down below the level of the seedheads, you are entering a different world, a parallel universe of secret wet places, unfathomable paths, rich with wet-loving life – and its predator.

The bittern is the sneaking predator of the reedbeds: creeping around with a dagger bill, eager to take eels, frogs, young birds. And when it is time to breed, and the male bittern's blood is stirring within him, then he makes his ghostly, far-carrying, foghorn cry. You can hear it from a mile off on a still morning, when nothing else is moving.

There is something primeval about it – a call that doesn't seem to be part of modern life. In a sense, it isn't. Bitterns are yet another bird that came close to extinction as breeding birds in this country. Reedbeds are not part of modern 21st-century life. Reeds are no longer much harvested, because most cottages are no longer thatched and, anyway, most thatch is imported these days. Reedbeds are not created spontaneously any more, because rivers and coasts are controlled with sea defences, and carefully maintained banks.

So the few reedbeds we have left are throwbacks. And they are lovingly maintained by conservation organisations. Reedbeds require constant work, or they dry up, and become patches of scrub. The bittern likes its reedbeds to be young and wet, and the challenge for conservationists is to keep their surviving reedbeds forever young.

In ancient times, before the draining of the Fens, there were far more reedbeds and, therefore, far more bitterns. A May night in the Fens would have been a 360-degree boom time; it must have been one of the great concerts in the history of the world. But we can still hear its ghost, still hear its echo, if we go to the right nature reserve. Minsmere in Suffolk, is one such place; Leighton Moss in Lancashire, Titchwell in Norfolk, are more. Along East Suffolk, there is a chain of reedbeds looked after by different conservation organisations and here, too, the bittern can be heard.

And occasionally, if you are dead lucky, the bittern can be seen: mostly in flight, generally low over the reeds, big flappy wings, neck tucked in, so that it looks like a big owl, landing with a sudden rather undignified flop. Occasionally, you can see one at work on the edge of the reeds, picking its way across its soggy domain, preoccupied, fussy, thick-necked, and rather chunky. In winter they can turn up unexpectedly at all sorts of wet places, as the young birds seek life, and adventure, and food, and a territory for themselves for the following spring.

But it is in the reedy reserves that you have your best chance of finding your bittern. It is something worth waiting for, worth having a long sit with your ears open. I recall one dawn, in the reedbeds a few miles north of Minsmere, with a friend who records bird sound. We were in a scrubby copse, overlooking, by a few feet, a vast area of reedbeds. And for an hour we had one of the great song-fests – behind us, nightingale, and before us, bittern. Not all the great concerts belong to the past.

The boom: that strange foghorn of the reeds, so full of a vanished world, and all we have lost. But, at the same time, it is a call filled with hope, for there are more bittern about than there have been for years. Some of the things we have lost we have found again. The bittern is back. And booming.

50. Peregrine falcon

Have I saved the best till last? In a sense, yes. In another sense, no. All birds are great, and all birds can supply a watching human with moments of enthralment, and magic, and delight. But for sheer drama, a peregrine is hard to top.

There has always been a mystique about the peregrine. It goes back deep into our history: a peregrine was the greatest falcon a great man could own. A nobleman with a peregrine on his wrist was like a film star with a Ferrari.

Peregrines are flashy all right, but it's all about performance. Peregrines are, simply enough, the fastest birds in the world – probably the fastest thing that has ever flown under its own power.

Peregrine falcon
Where to look: *wild, rocky country; increasingly in towns*
When to look: *all year, but most easily seen in spring, at known nest sites*
What to look for: *jet-fighter silhouette, stoops on prey like the wrath of god*
What to listen for: *harsh cackling near nest*

How fast? Well, the highest estimate I have seen gives them a top speed of 410 kph. Even if you halve that – perhaps more reasonably – it is still shockingly fast.

The bird hits top speed in a stoop – a falconry term for the flat-out plummet it makes onto its victims below. If you watch a peregrine, you will see it change abruptly from swift, direct, straight-and-level flight into – without any apparent preparation – a stoop: a headlong dive. Its body makes the famous falconine anchor shape in the air; it adds to its speed with it wings, and it comes down on its prey like a small bolt of thunder.

Mostly, its prey is birds, and they mostly die of shock. They never knew what hit them, and, presumably, still don't. Peregrines have a special fondness for pigeons, but they are by no means bigoted in the matter: 117 species have been recorded as peregrine prey, in this country alone.

Peregrines never quite went extinct in Britain, holding on in the rocky and remote places they love best. They are birds that can be hard to see; they cover a big range, they are swift and powerful fliers, and if you just go to a decent place, where peregrines are known to be about, you might get lucky, and then again, you might not.

But you can make a pilgrimage to Symonds Yat in

Gloucestershire. Here, at a spectacular site above the River Wye – peregrines have a profound taste for the spectacular – you can watch peregrines on the nest from April to August. There is even a telescope for you to look through.

So there it is: the most dramatic bird in Britain, and there for you on a plate, as it were. And if you think that detracts from the mystery, go anyway, and learn the bird, and get its shape, and its movements, and its vibes into your brain. And then, when you walk in the wilder places, you will know a peregrine when you see one, and thrill to the wildness of it all.

Peregrines are strong and purposeful fliers, even their glides look fierce and determined, unlike the airy nonchalance of the red kite. You can often see one without seeing one. A sudden explosion of alarm from a group of resting or feeding birds, and the air is suddenly filled with flying birds, and alarm calls, and mass panic, and you know something terrible has passed by. And often, in the right places, that means a peregrine.

There is a place I know in Cornwall, called, appropriately enough, Seagull Gully. Every now and then, it is as if someone had thrown a stick of dynamite into the place – a great rising fountain of birds and a cacophonous din. And if you are quick, and lucky, you can see the falcon, sometimes with a dead thing dangling beneath, at other times empty-taloned – but you can still imagine a rather smug look on his face, from causing all that havoc.

Peregrines are perhaps the ultimate pilgrimage bird, and they are an inspiration. An inspiration to carry on, to see more birds, to enjoy birds more, to enjoy life more. If the fastest bird that has ever lived can be seen, and by you, then how much more is within your scope? I hope this book has helped you, just a little, to open your eyes, open your ears, and allowed you to expand your range of possibilities. I hope, above all, that you can now let the birds come to you. Once you have birds with you, you will always have them.

That's what I hope, anyway. And the more people who hope so, the more likely we are to be right.

Where to find your pilgrimage birds

This list is by no means exhaustive, but these are the easiest places for a pilgrimage. All save Slimbridge (Bewick's swan) are operated by the RSPB, who will give more information should you require it. Please understand that not all the birds are at each of the sites all year round.

43. Avocet
Minsmere, Near Westleton, Suffolk
IP17 3BY
01728 648281, minsmere@rspb.org.uk
Grid reference TM 474672

Blacktoft Sands, East Riding of Yorkshire
01405 704665, blacktoft.sands@rspb.org.uk
Grid reference SE 845230

Exe Estuary, Near Exeter, Devon
01392 824614
Grid reference SX 960870

44. Osprey
Loch Garten, which is hard by Abernethy Forest, near Boat of Garten, Highland
01479 821409, abernethy@rspb.org.uk
Grid reference NH951190

Insh, Highland
01540 661518
Grid reference NH800020

45. Bewick's Swan

Wildfowl and Wetlands Trust
Slimbridge, Gloucestershire
GL2 7BT
0870 334 4000, www.wwt.org.uk
info.slimbridge@wwt.org.uk

Ouse Washes, Welches Dam
Manea, March, Cambridgeshire
01354 680212
Grid reference TL471860

46. Marsh Harrier

Minsmere (see avocet for details)
Blacktoft Sands (see avocet for details)

Leighton Moss
Near Carnforth, Leighton Moss
01524 701601, leightonmoss@rspb.org.uk

47. Gannet

Bempton, East Riding of Yorkshire
01262 851179
Grid reference TA 198735

48. Red Kite

Ynys-hir, Near Eglwys-fach
Cardiganshire
01654 700222, ynys-hir@rspb.org.uk

Other non-reserve places where red kites can be seen are in
the text of the chapter

49. Bittern

Minsmere (see avocet for details)

Leighton Moss (see marsh harrier for details

Titchwell, Norfolk
01485 210 779
titchwell@rspb.org.uk
Grid reference TF 758447

50. Peregrine falcon

Symond's Yat, Gloucestershire
01594 562 852

South Stack Cluffs, Holyhead
Anglesey
01407 764 973
Grid reference SH 218 827

The RSPB and the Royal Parks also operate a viewing station
where peregrines can be seen in central London. This operate
when the falcons nest during June and July. It can be found just
to the right of the York Gate entrance of Regent's Park. For
more details contact the RSPB.

Contacts

Royal Society
for the Protection of Birds
The Lodge
Sandy
Bedfordshire
SG19 2DL
017676 80551
www.rspb.org.uk

Worldwide Fund
for Nature
Panda House
Weyside Park
Godalming
Surrey
GU7 1XR
01483 426444
www.wwf-uk.org

Birdlife International
(an international
organisation for bird
conservation)
3-4 Wellbrook Court
Girton
Cambridge
CB3 0NA
01223 277318
www.birdlife.org.uk

The Wildlife Trusts
(Umbrella organisation for
the county wildlife trusts)
The Kiln
Waterside
Mather Road
Newark
Nottinghamshire
NG24 1WT
www.wildlifetrusts.org

Wildsounds
(a commercial organisation
that supplies recordings of
bird sound, other recordings
of natural sounds; also
wildlife books)
Roses Pightle
Cross St
Salthouse
NR25 7XH
www.wildsounds.com

Acknowledgements

A bad birdwatcher soon learns to seek the advice of a good birdwatcher. I have done better than that: for the purposes of this book, I had the great privilege of assistance from Rob Hume, who is a *great* birdwatcher: editor of the RSPB's Birds magazine, former chairman of the British Birds Rarities Committee, author of dozens of books on bird identification. It is entirely thanks to him that this book actually knows what it is talking about. He also contributed some of the jokes: a great man.

Thanks too for Peter Partington, who has given us drawings of birds as they live, as we see them: not dead skins. Refer to a conventional field guide for detail: Peter's drawings will give you a sense of the birds as living things. They will help you not just to see birds, but to understand them.

I would also like to add very special thanks to everyone at Short Books: through them, I re-found my faith in publishers. Enough said: so double-thanks to Georgina Capel for bringing us together.

Finally, thanks to the companion with whom I saw my first avocet and my first marsh harrier. Reader, I married her. You would, wouldn't you?

Also published by Short Books:

THE GOOD GRANNY GUIDE
Or how to be a modern grandmother
Jane Fearnley-Whittingstall

As all good grandparents know, the most precious gift they can offer their grandchildren is time.

In *The Good Granny Guide*, you will find a whole range of practical advice to help you make the most of the time you spend with your grandchildren.

Jane Fearnley-Whittingstall, an enthusiastic and closely involved grandmother of four, has gathered first-hand tips from other grandparents and their families in many different situations. The result is a hugely insightful handbook − a wonderful resource of wisdom, history and humour − covering everything from childcare trouble-shooting to what NOT to say to the daughter-in-law.

£12.99   ISBN 1-9040977-08-1

TEACHER ON THE RUN
True Tales of Classroom Chaos
Francis Gilbert

Gilbert is back and he's glad to be back. After three years of teaching at Truss, an inner-city sink school, Francis Gilbert has been offered a job in the English department at his old school, a nice suburban comprehensive. Like a prisoner out of Colditz, he feels like he's just landed a job in toytown.

But, with Mr Morgan, the deaf old English teacher, still cackling, the staff room politics in tatters, alarming complaints from the parents and, worst of all, the memories of his own disturbed childhood suddenly rushing back at him, how long can Gilbert's dreamland last?

£9.99   ISBN   1-904977-03-0

WINNER OF THE MIND BOOK OF THE YEAR
AWARD 2005

The Cruel Mother
A Family Ghost Laid to Rest
Siân Busby

In 1919 Siân Busby's great-grandmother, Beth, gave birth
to triplets. One of the babies died at birth and eleven days
later Beth drowned the surviving twins in a bath of cold
water. She was sentenced to an indefinite term of impris-
onment at Broadmoor.

The murder and the deep sense of shame it generated
obviously affected Beth, her husband and their surviving
children to an extraordinary degree, but it also resounded
through the lives of her grandchildren and great-grandchil-
dren. In Siân's case, ill-suppressed knowledge of the event
manifested itself in recurring nightmares and contributed
towards a prolonged bout of post-natal depression. After
the birth of her second son, she decided to investigate the
story once and for all and lay to rest the ghosts which have
haunted the family for 80 years...

1-904095-06-5   £7.99

"A gripping tale of madness and infanticide during
the Great War... Powerful and disturbing"
Margaret Forster

ducks in a row
An A-Z of Offlish

The definitive guide to the language of Office English

Carl Newbrook

Ducks in a Row is a dictionary and guidebook to the new and absurd language of Office English, or Offlish – workplace slang, common jargon, bogus phrases and all the myriad ridiculous idioms that we use to impress and confuse our colleagues and to climb the greasy pole of corporate advancement.

It is a book to delight, amuse, instruct and entertain anyone who has ever worked in, or ever will work in, an office.

1-904977-35-9   £9.99